Sculpting the Buddha Within

SCULPTING THE BUDDHA WITHIN

The Life and Thought of Shinjo Ito

Shuri Kido, Poet

Wisdom Publications
199 Elm Street
Somerville, MA 02144 USA
wisdompubs.org

Library of Congress Cataloging-in-Publication Data
Names: Kido, Shuri, 1959– author.
Title: Sculpting the Buddha within: the life and thought of Shinjo Ito / Shuri Kido.
Identifiers: LCCN 2019000218 (print) | LCCN 2019011027 (ebook) |
    ISBN 9781614296300 (ebook) | ISBN 9781614296195 (pbk.: alk. paper)
Subjects: LCSH: Ito, Shinjo, 1906–1989. | Buddhists—Japan—Biography. |
    Buddhist priests—Japan—Biography. | Shinnyo-en—Biography. | Acalanatha-
    Vidyaraja (Buddhist deity)—Cult—Japan. | Buddhist cults—Japan—History—
    20th century. | Buddhism—Japan—History—20th century.
Classification: LCC BQ964.T6 (ebook) | LCC BQ964.T6 K53 2019 (print) |
    DDC 294.3/92 [B] —dc23
LC record available at https://lccn.loc.gov/2019000218

ISBN 978-1-61429-619-5   ebook ISBN 978-1-61429-630-0

23 22 21 20 19   5 4 3 2 1

Cover design by Jim Zaccaria. Interior design by Greta D. Sibley. Set in Garamond
Premier Pro.

MIX
Paper from
responsible sources
FSC® C005010

Please visit fscus.org.

Creating a buddha image is not about sculpting the form.
It is said that all beings possess a buddha nature, and
I sculpt buddha images out of a wish to make each
individual a living buddha.

—*Shinjo Ito*

Contents

Foreword

In Remembrance of Shinjo Ito

PRIOR TO HIS RETURN TO the eternal abode of all awakened ones, Shinnyo-en's founding Dharma master, Shinjo Ito, spent his entire life in the sacred pursuit of guiding as many people as possible onto a path of solace and well-being.

In my view, the existence of religion itself stems from our fundamental acknowledgment of forces that transcend the human condition, whether natural or what we call deities or buddhas. It is my understanding that Master Shinjo began his religious pursuits after having mastered a form of spiritual discernment known as the *Byozeisho*, a divinatory tradition handed down in his native land of Kai (present-day Yamanashi). I believe one of the purposes of Buddhism is to teach us to live in alignment with the forces of nature, within whose interwoven web all life thrives. So I was particularly impressed by Master Shinjo's insight to first study the principles of our natural world before training in the Buddhadharma.

No matter how much we may ponder heaven, earth, the divine, or celestial bodies, though, the ultimate truths of the cosmos far exceed the scope of human understanding. Yet it is Buddhism's mission to pass on such wisdom to succeeding generations. I believe we can only do so by returning to its core truths without being fixated on minutiae.

Buddhism talks of the preciousness of transmitting the Buddha's teachings to impart the means to spiritual liberation, peace, and tranquility to those caught up in the complexities of our world. Saicho, the great founder of the Tendai tradition, taught of selfless devotion in service to others. I feel Master Shinjo—faithful to the very essence of spiritual practice from the inception of his sangha—also prioritized the genuine liberation and awakening of individuals over the growth of his community. His accomplishments speak to a spirit that was truly the same as the ultimate intentions of all the buddhas upon whose images we meditate and was in keeping with the path realized through their many protections.

I would like to convey my deepest respect for Master Shinjo's efforts that have brought many people together. I am simultaneously filled with great sorrow that he did not live longer. I have no doubt he would still be working vigorously toward his goals were he still with us today.

I encourage each of you—as his successors—to unfailingly cherish, embody, and actively carry his legacy into the future for the spiritual liberation and awakening of humankind. This, I am convinced, is both the mission of his sangha and the greatest way to repay the kindness of your founding master.

Most Venerable Etai Yamada (1895–1994)
Former Head of Enryakuji Monastery, Mount Hiei, Japan
Tendai Buddhism

Preface

BUDDHISM IS UNDERSTOOD TO HAVE originated 2,500 years ago in India with the teachings of its founder, Siddhartha Gautama, also known as Buddha Shakyamuni. The religion evolved as it spread from the Indian subcontinent through Central, East, and Southeast Asia.

A basic tenet of the Buddhist teachings is that nothing is fixed or permanent and that change is natural. This is especially true when it comes to adapting the path of practice for different individuals or cultures. The Buddha himself was very accommodating of the needs of his disciples—particularly those from different places or diverse groups in society—and he allowed for adjustments to the way in which his teachings were presented. As a result, Buddhism became a tradition that adapted to the needs of the people it served, and over the course of twenty-five centuries numerous reformers have founded different schools and sects of Buddhism to meet such evolving needs.

This book is the story of one such person, Shinjo Ito (1906–1989). Shinjo was the founder of Shinnyo-en, a lay Buddhist order based on Shingon Buddhism. He was born in Yamanashi Prefecture in Japan. He started his career as an aeronautical engineer, but soon felt a strong calling to pursue Buddhism and dedicate himself to a religious life. He trained at Daigoji, a monastery of the Shingon sect of esoteric Buddhism in Kyoto, and became a great acharya—a Dharma master authorized to establish a separate denomination if he chose to do so. In 1946, after wartime restrictions on religious orders were abolished, the spiritual community that Shinjo founded became officially independent of Shingon Buddhism. Shinjo named his new group Makoto Kyodan (Sangha of Truth) and established the community that would later come to be called Shinnyo-en.

Key to Shinjo's calling to found a new order was that adherents be truly enriched by the promise of Buddhism—in other words, that they find more than temporary benefit and walk a path for personal transformation into a more selfless, joyful, and compassionate person. He did not want his followers to come to him just for relief from their everyday problems. Shinjo became deeply devoted to developing a path by which people could improve their journey in life as well as contribute to the happiness of others. This devotion also expressed the noble vow of a bodhisattva, a person dedicated to walking the path to enlightenment for the sake of all beings.

After years of exploring and reading the great body of teachings in the Buddhist canon, Shinjo found the doctrinal basis he was looking for in the *Nirvana Sutra*. Shinjo used the principles and concepts of the *Nirvana Sutra* to develop a lay Buddhist practice devoted to attaining the spiritual freedom that comes from cultivating one's buddha nature (the potential to be awakened) and experiencing the timeless nature of buddhahood. Shinjo found in the teachings of the *Nirvana Sutra* a positive message of hope, one of discovering within oneself a goodness that is expressed in ordinary life and that can then be transformed into sublime peace and happiness. This was exactly what Shinjo had been hoping to bring to his community.

In Shingon esoteric Buddhism, the central figure representing ultimate awakening is called Mahavairochana (Jpn. Dainichi). This archetypal buddha represents the dharmakaya, or "dharma body," of the Buddha. In other words, he is a personification of the highest ideals of the Buddhist teachings. Shakyamuni, the historical Buddha, does not hold a central place in that tradition, as he is regarded as having been merely a nirmanakaya, or "emanation body" of the ultimate in Buddhism. Shakyamuni is regarded as having appeared in the form of flesh and blood for those who lacked the spiritual ability to see and interact with the dharma body.

The fact that Shinjo was a practitioner of Shingon esoteric Buddhism but made the Mahayana version of the *Nirvana Sutra*—the *Mahaparinirvana Sutra*, which is considered to convey Shakyamuni's final teachings—his foundational text shows that he did not limit himself to the transcendent, esoteric Buddhist means of awakening. He instead drew attention once again to the flesh-and-blood teacher—the historical Buddha—who lived among other people and worked within the flow of human history and society.

Shinjo's new branch of esoteric Buddhism is a distinct denomination called the Shinnyo Samaya stream and focuses on a lay form of practice grounded in the essentials that underlie monastic training. It represents Shinjo's answer as a Buddhist teacher to the question of what Buddhism should be like in the increasingly complex and diverse modern culture of the twentieth century in which he lived. In recognition of the achievement of founding a new order, in 1966 Shinjo's parent monastery, Daigoji, awarded him the highest title of a fully ordained monk, and in 1997, eight years after Shinjo had passed away, it erected the Shinnyo Samaya Hall on its grounds in recognition of his achievements.

As Shinjo deepened his understanding of the *Nirvana Sutra*, he felt compelled to express what he felt from it through the medium of sculpture and decided to craft an original image of a reclining Buddha delivering his final teaching just before passing into timeless nirvana. Beginning with the sculpting of this first nirvana image, Shinjo dedicated himself to sculpting various types of Buddhist imagery that he felt could help people connect to their own buddha nature. The copious number of his works helped him to become known as one of the preeminent Buddhist masters and sculptors of the twentieth century. In August 2006, the centennial of Shinjo Ito's birth, an exhibition at the Tokyo Art Club entitled "Centennial Exhibition: The Vision and Craft of Shinjo Ito" was opened to the public and his Buddhist sculptures and other works were put on display.

The original edition of this book in Japanese (by Chuokoron-Shinsha) was a result of that initiative to commemorate the centennial of Shinjo Ito's birth. That edition was edited by the Shinjo Publication Committee, which consisted of five members: myself (Shuri Kido, poet), Yasuaki Nara (professor emeritus of Indian Buddhist philosophy, Komazawa University), the Most Venerable Junna Nakada (The 103rd chief abbott of Daigoji Monastery), Masahiro Shimoda (professor of Indian philosophy and Buddhist studies at the graduate school of the University of Tokyo), and the Reverend Mitsuo Nagatsuka (executive director of Shinnyo-en). The committee sought in the book's pages to trace the course of Shinjo's life as well as his thought and practice as a Buddhist master. Aside from Reverend Mitsuo Nagatsuka, none of the other members of the committee were members of Shinnyo-en. The committee was assembled in this way so that this book would offer a profile of the Buddhist master Shinjo Ito from an external perspective. I was extremely surprised that a religious group would plan something like that at all.

In addition to a biography of Shinjo Ito, the Japanese edition of this work contained scholarly essays that discussed the connection between Shakyamuni and Shinjo's Buddhist community and the significance of that connection. It also addressed the evolution of Buddhism as reflected in the teachings of the *Nirvana Sutra*, and provided an essay on Shinjo and the significance of his teachings in terms of Japanese Buddhism. These scholarly essays, when combined with the official biography of Shinjo, constituted a fine volume that introduced the character of Shinjo as well as the historical and doctrinal context of his teachings.

Initially, we had hoped to hire a professional biographer to produce the biographical portion of the book, but after failing to find a suitable candidate, the work of crafting a critical biography about Shinjo Ito fell to me. I was taken aback at being assigned the task, as I did not have a deep knowledge of Shinjo Ito or Shinnyo-en, nor did I feel that I had an adequate understanding of Buddhism. How, therefore, could I write a critical biography of a Buddhist who had established a new order?

After accepting responsibility for the task, with some apprehension I began my work of putting together as thorough a biography of the man as I could. I based my work on Shinjo's personal diaries and interviews with those who had known him personally. I also began to study everything I could about Buddhism and the traditions from which Shinjo drew his inspiration. I read some of the best-known Buddhist sutras, such as the *Nirvana Sutra*, all of the works of the great master Kukai, and books by prominent Buddhist writers such as Dr. Hajime Nakamura, taking notes as I read each source. I also carefully read the writings of Shinjo Ito.

My research took almost two years, during which time I received a tremendous amount of assistance from Shinnyo-en. I was even given an as-yet-unpublished memoir of Shinjo Ito that contained precious records from when the order was established and around the period that it was subjected to religious persecution. Reading his personal journals and memoirs, I felt as if I had met Shinjo himself. I think it was then that I knew the angle I needed to take to write an objective biography.

I knew that my biography could not simply cover well-known events such as Shinjo's decision to establish Shinnyo-en after his encounter with a thirteenth-century Achala statue made by the Japanese sculptor Unkei, his entry into the Buddhist priesthood and his training at Daigoji, his parting from the Shingon school to form his own denomination after the Second World War, his adoption of the *Nirvana Sutra* as the doctrinal pivot after experiencing religious persecution, or the creation of the Great Parinirvana image. Every practicing member of Shinnyo-en was already well aware of such events; simply tracing them would not make for an engaging biography from an outsider's perspective.

Aside from the fact that most of the major events of Shinjo's life were common knowledge to practitioners of the Shinnyo-en path, I had my own questions and curiosities about how and why things went the way they did in his life. Why did he choose to do his initial training in the Shingon school founded by the great master Kukai? And why, of all the Shingon temples and monasteries, did he choose Daigoji for that purpose? The Buddhism practiced in the Shingon sect is of course based on the *Mahavairochana* and *Vajrasekhara* sutras, which are considered the ultimate teachings of esoteric Buddhism. So why did Shinjo Ito turn to the *Nirvana Sutra* and make it the backbone of his new denomination when it is considered part of the Mahayana Buddhist canon and not, strictly speaking, regarded as part of esoteric Buddhism (Mikkyo) in Japan? The biography that I created seeks answers to these questions.

Shinjo did not set out with the goal of systematizing Buddhism in some different way. He did, however, put his own thoughts and beliefs into writing. And rather than encourage his followers to believe in a fixed system of practice or beliefs, he took a different approach, one of working diligently to cultivate, or sculpt, a buddha in the hearts of his followers.

The metaphoric phrase "three bows for every strike of the chisel" (Jpn. *itto sanrai*) is sometimes used at Shinnyo-en to describe the devoted, reverent nature of Shinjo's efforts to encourage and guide individuals, especially in reference to the sculptural works he fashioned to inspire people to see and bring out the buddha nature within themselves. Each encounter he had with practitioners, each individual teaching he gave to help his followers on the path to inner peace, was followed up with devotion and care.

Shinjo was not interested in establishing something new for the sake of fame or for his own elevation in status. He took his work as a mentor and teacher to heart. The expression "three bows for every strike of the chisel" describes the humble passion he brought to his leadership, which is also reflected in the magnificent reclining Buddha statue that he sculpted. In creating this biography, I chose to pay special attention to the very human aspects of Shinjo, allowing those who may place him on a pedestal to see him as the husband, father, founder, and fellow human being that he was.

After I completed my work, I asked the ordained member on the publication committee to read through it and check my use of Buddhist terminology, concepts, and Pali and Sanskrit terms. I made many improvements based on his feedback. I also asked Shinnyo-en's Reverend Mitsuo Nagatsuka to specifically check the history and terminology related to Shinnyo-en to ensure that it was correct. My biography of Shinjo Ito filled around 380 sheets of standard writing paper, and I wrote it in a little over three weeks. I paid the price for such concentrated work with such terrible back pain that I had to see a chiropractor. The chiropractor informed me that I had sprained my pelvis. That helped me remember that even my hipbone has joints! Such recollections invoke nostalgia for me now.

Today, more than a decade after the centennial celebration of his birth, Shinjo's teachings have continued to spread throughout the world, taking root in countries historically unfamiliar with Buddhism or the life of Shinjo Ito. Current adherents of the Shinnyo-en path will certainly be familiar with Shinjo's daughter Shinso Ito, the head priest of Shinchoji and the head of Shinnyo-en since Shinjo's passing. But the life and thought of Shinjo still creatively influences the tradition he founded: his magnificent sculptures of the Buddha in repose are displayed in Shinnyo-en temples, for example. Shinjo himself, in the form of relief sculptures, photographs, or busts, is present as well.

Those who knew Shinjo, who knew his remarkable spirit, warmth, and generosity, remain, and stories about him still circulate within the tradition he founded. And whenever I hear Shinso Ito speak, I see that the teachings of Shinjo and his wife and coleader Tomoji Ito live on, transforming to suit each new era. This is surely what it means to pass on Buddhism through a chain of teachers and students. It is only natural that the members of the Shinnyo-en community who inherit and live these teachings are interested in learning more about Shinjo, his struggles, his triumphs, his losses, and the peace that he found on his path.

And so now, you hold in your hands some further answers for the curious. This new edition of the work—the first of its kind to come out in another language besides Japanese—is more than a simple translation of the original work published by Chuokoron-Shinsha. With the help of a dedicated group of people, it has been restructured for the wider international audience to create a wholly original version released by Wisdom Publications. For example, in this edition we chose to pare away the supplemental scholarly support and explanations in order to focus more squarely on the life of Shinjo Ito, much of it told in his own words. I am greatly indebted to all those who have contributed to make this book possible.

The aim of the original Japanese edition was a diverse volume that could provide a deeper understanding of both Shinjo and Buddhism itself. The aim of this new English edition is to concentrate on more fully capturing the life of a twentieth-century Buddhist reformer who sculpted buddha images with his own hands and who sought to shape the Buddha within the hearts of ordinary people. If this English edition manages to achieve that, and if it becomes an inspiration or guiding light for people in an age of confusion, nothing would make this author happier.

—*Shuri Kido*

Introduction

Shinjo's Nirvana Sutra—*The Practice of Shinnyo*

THE ORIGINAL JAPANESE EDITION OF *Shinjo: Sculpting the Buddha Within* was published on the centennial of the birth of Shinjo Ito (1906–1989), the founder of Shinnyo-en. Ten years later, to commemorate the 110th anniversary of his birth, an expanded version was released in paperback to bring it to a wider audience as a new addition to the time-honored Chuko Paperback Library (published by Chuokoron-Shinsha), in which this essay first appeared.

After Shinjo's passing, I succeeded him as the spiritual head of Shinnyo-en and chief priest of the Tokeizan Shinchoji temple. As such, I was asked by the publications committee to contribute an essay to this wonderful biography written by the poet Shuri Kido. My task in this newly expanded edition is to describe Shinjo's perspective on the *Nirvana Sutra* and the essence of his exploration, centering on *shinnyo,* a key Buddhist concept.

Since this expanded edition is published outside of Shinnyo-en, I was concerned that my participation as a contributor would undermine its objectivity. At the same time, having known the founder in close proximity for longer than anyone else during his rigorously devoted life, I thought I might be able to offer a unique portrait of

Shinjo, the founder and master of a particular spiritual path. Accordingly, I agreed to the request and took up my pen.

Shinjo's Nirvana Image

Shinjo Ito used the Mahayana version of the *Nirvana Sutra*—the *Mahaparinirvana Sutra*—as the primary doctrinal basis for Shinnyoen. In 1956 he began writing a series of commentaries on the sutra entitled "The Last Teachings" in the internal publication *Kangi Sekai* (Joyous World). That same year, he resolved to sculpt an image of the reclining Buddha and built a prototype that measured 79 centimeters in length. In January of the following year, he started work and created a 5-meter-long image of the Buddha entering nirvana that is today housed at our head temple complex in Tachikawa, Tokyo.

This sculpture shows clearly what the *Nirvana Sutra* meant to Shinjo. For him the sutra was no mere literary text but a living expression of shinnyo, the positive energy of awakening reality. Art was one way that Shinjo gave concrete expression to principles in the *Nirvana Sutra*, and so I'd say his creations were works of shinnyo.

As a religious leader and founder of a spiritual path, the creative act was for Shinjo an act of prayer and meditation. Sculpting images and making calligraphic carvings was also simply an expression of his natural talent. He produced many sculptures of the Buddha entering nirvana and other Buddhist images based on esoteric Buddhist tradition and the principles of the *Nirvana Sutra*, creatively fusing the artistic traditions of East and West. He longed "to sculpt the latent Buddha within the heart of every person," and he expressed that desire spiritually through his work.

When Shinjo first announced that he intended to create a nirvana image (a reclining Buddha about to pass away and enter eternal nirvana), I and everyone around him was surprised, including his wife and then head of the sangha, Tomoji. Shinjo had previously created a buddha image in the form of a wooden relief of Fudo (Achala), but this was the first time that he had taken on the challenge of creating such a large Buddhist sculpture. It should be noted that statues of the reclining Buddha were uncommon in Japan, although images of the reclining Buddha were fairly common in paintings. As for sculptures, Shinjo's only previous experience was sculpting busts of his two sons Kyodoin and Shindoin. They were my elder brothers, both of whom died young.

In 1953, just before the first anniversary of the death of Shindoin, a sculptor came to visit and told us that he had had a strange dream indicating that he should go to Shinnyo-en. Shinjo told him there was something he wanted to create and gave him a photograph of Shindoin. Sometime later the sculptor returned with a bust to be used as a prototype. However, neither my mother nor I could see much of a resemblance to my brother. We felt his conscientious nature wasn't quite captured.

Shinjo asked the sculptor, "Can you allow me two weeks to add some touches to this?" He gave his all to the work, not stopping until he was satisfied, and it was then that the real face of Shindoin appeared.

The sculptor exclaimed, "This is your work, Master Shinjo. I really admire what you've done to it!"

For Shinjo, sculpting was also a process of catharsis and healing, a time for quiet contemplation and dialogue with his late sons, allowing him ultimately to come to terms with the pain of losing them.

As a result, beautiful sculptures were created. We could say that with the images of his sons, Shinjo created bodhisattva figures whose clear gazes contained something universal—the light of shinnyo.

Shinjo made progress on the nirvana image with the help of Tomoji, some practitioners who were professional carpenters, and his closest disciples. All of his helpers were amateurs, however, with little prior experience in sculpting or casting. Nevertheless, all of them trusted Shinjo implicitly and gave him their full support. I also helped with transporting materials, removing impurities from the plaster we made, and various other tasks.

Shinjo was originally an aeronautical engineer, a man of originality and ingenuity. For example, he used a barrel to create the framework for the sculpture, and divided up the huge figure into sections that he could work on individually. He invented his own tools to cut and smooth clay that were made of hard piano wire, based on a design he had drawn up himself. When experts saw these tools, they marveled at their functionality.

The work began in earnest on January 2 of the new year 1957, and despite the intense cold and the bloody, cracked skin of his fingers due to the sculpting process, Shinjo immersed himself in working on the statue. He literally forgot to sleep and eat, forgot whether it was day or night, and on March 18 the 5-meter plaster figure was completed.

Shinjo had been a talented photographer since his teens, and he spoke of his work on the statue in terms of photography: "When you take a photo, first you look through the viewfinder, and then you use the lens to focus on your subject. Similarly, when I sculpt a buddha image the subject comes into focus as I cut and shape the clay. It's like something is telling me what to do. The Buddha emerges and is made lifelike naturally. This is how the statue was finished in just seventy days." He added, "When I was sculpting the face, the facial features seemed to appear in my mind's eye. So I simply placed the clay over that form. Of course there was a prototype, but once I set to work I completed it hardly referring back to the model I had made."

Shinjo learned from the work of traditional Buddhist sculptors like Jocho (d. 1057) and Unkei (c. 1150–1223). He also sought out examples of Gandharan Buddhist statues and Greek and Roman sculpture. He wanted to express in his Buddha statue the human wisdom, compassion, nobility, and warmth of both Eastern and Western spiritual traditions. Perhaps as a result of that attempt, the statue's face appears to transcend ethnicity and gender. People can see in the Buddha's expression—so full of love—their own fathers, mothers, children, siblings, teachers, or friends.

In the earliest period of Indian Buddhist sculpture, artists depicted the Buddha's seat, but not the Buddha himself. His presence could only be hinted at through symbols such as the sun wheel or a lotus blossom. That is not to say that the Buddha was never figuratively represented. Pious practitioners would often see their own form or interpretation of the Buddha in the empty seat. That was the beauty of having the empty seat.

The *Nirvana Sutra* differs from earlier sutras in that it sets out Buddhist teachings in positive terms—*shunyata* (nonsubstantiality, or emptiness) becomes *non-shunyata* (substantiality, or fullness) and *no-self* becomes *self.*

The traditional concepts of *buddha, buddhahood,* or *buddha nature* as being about emptiness or nonsubstantiality are understood in the *Nirvana Sutra* not as detached states of being but as states grasped subjectively through direct intuitive experience. By having people look at tangible forms of the Buddha or buddhahood, in this case his nirvana image, Shinjo wanted viewers of his artwork to be inspired to see the unseen buddhahood all around and within themselves—as well as the latent buddha nature in themselves and others. That is how he felt people can create a world of joy in their everyday lives, and this is why he continued to create buddha images.

For Shinjo, creating Buddhist statues was an act of seeking the way, and sharing what he created was a method of helping people find awakening and spiritual liberation. I remember how Shinjo would enter into a deep state of mutual resonance with the essence of the buddhas he was sculpting. He sculpted in this state of spiritual interpenetration in which the self and the buddha figure become one. In this state of oneness, at an invisible level there is no knowing where the boundary lies between the buddha and the self. We might call it a state in which one buddha sculpts another.

There is an expression, *yuibutsu yobutsu* (lit. "only one buddha after another"), which refers to the highest state you can reach, in which you are in a world of only buddhas. As a little girl, I believe this was what I witnessed—a world made up of only buddhas—while watching with a deep sense of awe my father and mother working through the night.

I believe Shinjo was aware of the great responsibility he was entrusted with as a *maha acharya* (great master) to keep turning the wheel of dharma. As such, he dedicated himself to the creation of Buddhist images, imbuing them with his focused prayer and meditation for the sake of others. After the images were finished, he would inspirit (consecrate) them himself, giving them a life of their own.

Likewise, when Shinjo performed rituals as the officiant, he would also become one with the qualities of the buddha figure at the center of the rite. This too was an act of awakening the buddha nature of the celebrants, leading to an experience of shinnyo for those participating.

Shinjo would complete a statue by smoothing and polishing it. Instead of looking slimmer, the statue seemed to look fuller the more he did so, and at the end it was as if it drew breath and came alive. Shinjo said, "My statues are an expression of my faith and conviction in the sacred. I put my soul into it as well as my prayer that all beings find peace and contentment." People say Shinjo's works create an atmosphere in which they experience buddha nature. At such moments they also engage in shaping the buddha within themselves.

A Timeless Presence

Traditionally, nirvana images depict the Buddha entering final nirvana at the age of eighty. Shinjo's image, however, has a very youthful countenance. This way of depicting the Buddha reflects what it says in the *Nirvana Sutra*—the true Buddha is a permanent and timeless presence (always present).

Shinjo explained his approach as follows: "The nirvana image portrays Shakyamuni at the time of his death, so if he were to be shown realistically, he should be portrayed as an old man. But when I began this work I had the image of the Buddha at the moment of his awakening imprinted on my mind, and it was that which I wanted to create. When he attained enlightenment, the Buddha reached a realm beyond the cycle of birth, death, and rebirth. And so I would say that he lives on today. This is why I thought his face should be that of the vibrant, young Buddha." Another way of putting this is to say that he found the Buddha to be forever present within the Dharma or principles put forth in the *Nirvana Sutra*.

Tomoji once explained the nature of the Buddhist sutras (lit. "threads" of teachings). She used the intriguing metaphor of an electric power network: "Just as electricity is transmitted from a power plant to a transformer substation, which then carries it to a home, the teachings of the Buddha are transmitted in a single line or current from person to person, soul to soul. The sutra contains the 'threads' or lines (lineages) that link people to happiness by leading them out of pain, sadness, and struggle."

Thanks to electricity we can banish darkness at the flick of a switch. Likewise, the Buddha's teachings can illuminate the darkness in our minds, allowing us to develop a broader, clearer field of vision. Just as electricity reaches us through transmission lines to light our houses, sutras have been conveyed through diverse streams or lineages in history over a span of 2,500 years to enlighten our hearts and minds in the present day.

Written versions of the sutras arose as a means to convey the Buddha's teachings only after they had been passed on orally for hundreds of years by the spiritual communities of monks and nuns, the sangha. Later, as the teachings spread to other lands, the courageous efforts of translators, who served as the "substations" in Tomoji's metaphor, ensured the transmission of teachings into other languages.

Electrical lines run in complex formations from transformer substations to the homes where people live. Yet nothing actually separates us from that power. Each home is directly connected to its source no matter how intricate the layout of the power lines and cables is. The sutras can be likened to this network of power lines.

The *Nirvana Sutra* is often characterized as an account of the events surrounding the death of the Buddha. Shinjo believed, however, that to read the sutra only in terms of the Buddha's death was to miss its essence. The main theme of the sutra is not the Buddha's death but the deathless quality of the Buddha. The World-Honored One—another way to refer to the Buddha—said to his disciples that they should not neglect their practice but always continue to be diligent in their spiritual efforts. He said that in reality he would not die but would always be with those who practiced the way, that he would live on forever within the teachings.

"Be a lamp unto yourself," he advised.

"Be a refuge unto yourself," he taught in order to encourage people to find spiritual refuge not externally but within themselves.

"Hold fast to the Dharma as a lamp." In other words, seek refuge in the Dharma.

In the Mahayana versions of the *Nirvana Sutra*, the phrase "lamp unto yourself" is understood as the buddha nature innate in everyone, while holding fast to "the Dharma as a lamp" refers to the buddha who is always present.

No matter what time period it may be, those who trust in and practice the teachings of the *Nirvana Sutra* can transcend time and space to feel what it must have been like when the Buddha gave his final teachings in the *sala* grove so long ago. Mahayana sutras are meant to be understood subjectively in this way, not literally. The state of *mahaparinirvana* (great nirvana) involves a shift in perspective about nirvana; it is to see it not as a negation but as an affirmation. For example, the Buddha's death does not signal that he is gone from us but rather that he is timeless and always present.

Whereas earlier accounts of the Buddha's death focused on impermanence and suffering, the Mahayana version presents his physical death in a new light—as pointing to the everlasting potential to find joy and happiness. Shinjo perceived that this was what the World-Honored One meant to teach. Within the impermanence of all things, we can also find an unchanging and priceless treasure within our own hearts and minds. In the Mahayana version of the *Nirvana Sutra*, this state of lasting joy is called *permanence-bliss-self-purity*.

A Modern-Day Chunda

If we think beyond time and space, in prayer or meditation we can place ourselves among the congregation of people who gathered at the sacred scene of the Buddha's *parinirvana*, or entry into the final state, one of complete nirvana free from the physical constraints of the body. In doing so, we too become the Buddha's spiritual heirs as we receive the final teachings of Shakyamuni, who is one emanation of the timeless dharma body. This is what Shinjo wanted to teach us by taking particular note of Chunda, from whom, in the sutra, the Buddha chose to receive the final offering.

As the parinirvana of the Buddha drew near, all beings—including kings, wealthy nobles, and bodhisattvas of great merit—gathered in Kushinagara to make a final offering. Yet from among all these supplicants the World-Honored One singled out a young layman, a blacksmith named Chunda who had hurried to that place with fifteen of his friends. While Chunda grieves at the impermanence of the Buddha's life on Earth because of his passing into final nirvana, he also maintains a firm belief in the Buddha's enduring presence and makes his offering to the timeless dharma body that transcends the physical form of the Buddha.

This scene where Chunda makes the last offering to the Buddha is depicted in the *Nirvana Sutra* chapter "Questions Raised by All Those Congregated": "At that time, everyone in the multitude, having brought offerings for the World-Honored One, awakened or strengthened their aspiration to pursue the Buddha's teachings toward unsurpassed enlightenment." This means that the merit of the good deed of Chunda's offering has spread beyond himself as an individual to the whole assembly, allowing each person there to awaken their own aspiration to pursue the way to enlightenment, or buddhahood.

Similarly, in the rituals of esoteric Buddhism, the officiant imagines himself or herself as the bodhisattva Vajrasattva (who symbolizes one aspiring toward buddhahood) and—on behalf of all the participants of the ritual—conducts the rite as an offering to the dharma-body form of the Buddha (dharmakaya Tathagata). In the *Nirvana Sutra* Chunda's offering represents all those seeing the Buddha off as he departs this world—and as a result, all who have congregated before the Buddha can have their aspirations and vows fulfilled.

In the *Nirvana Sutra* the Buddha often encouraged those asking him questions with words of praise such as, "Very good!" He accepted the offering Chunda made in a similarly encouraging manner. The same encouraging tone is a characteristic of the sutra itself. It teaches—through the narrative of the young layman Chunda—that everyone, regardless of ordination status or gender, can uphold and become an heir to the unsurpassed Dharma. The *Nirvana Sutra* chapter "Bodhisattva Highly Virtuous King" teaches that "a state without hindrances can be called nirvana." It is a state that transcends all barriers and is full of clarity, true freedom, and equality, where all distinctions cease to exist.

At any point in history, a person who sincerely practices the six paramitas (perfections)—generosity (*dana*), ethical discipline (*shila*), forebearance (*kshanti*), diligent effort or perseverance (*virya*), meditative contemplation (*dhyana*), and wisdom (*prajna*)—can become a Chunda as depicted in the *Nirvana Sutra*. Such a person transcends time, space, gender, age, and all other differences to experience the timeless buddhahood and inner freedom that are none other than the awakening described in the *Nirvana Sutra*.

Icchantikas Can Also Achieve Liberation

A buddha is an "awakened one." Therefore buddha nature is the basic nature of human beings that awakens them to their innate goodness. Put differently, it points to human potential.

The latter part of the *Nirvana Sutra* often reiterates the idea that buddha nature is the Middle Way. In the sutra the World-Honored One also describes buddha nature as *paramartha-shunyata*, meaning "paramount emptiness." *Paramartha* refers to ultimate truth or highest wisdom, while *shunyata* is to be "empty" of hindering delusions. It is to see the two sides of existence, of the negated *and* the affirmed—in other words, emptiness and nonemptiness, permanence and impermanence, suffering and bliss, self and nonself. The Middle Way requires that we consider both the emptiness and fullness of all things, both the self and nonself. The Buddha teaches that seeing one without the other would not be the path of the Middle Way, and concludes by equating the Middle Way with buddha nature.

Therefore wisdom in the context of paramount emptiness (*paramartha-shunyata*) is less about viewing contrasting phenomena as diametrically opposite and more about recognizing the opposing aspects, whether they be "empty" or "not empty" (*shunyata* or non-*shunyata*). Until the time the *Nirvana Sutra* came out, the idea of emptiness (*shunyata*) had been expressed in negative terms: as neither existence nor nonexistence. The *Nirvana Sutra*, however, builds on that understanding, using more affirmative expressions: as both existence and nonexistence—ultimately, all are embraced. This inclusiveness makes the *Nirvana Sutra* special. Indeed, living based on the wisdom of the *Nirvana Sutra*, what the Middle Way truly is, enables us to give full expression to our buddha nature.

This inclusiveness or affirmation can be seen not only in the sutra's description of buddha nature but also in its ideas on how to cultivate buddha nature. You might ask: How can one cultivate one's buddha nature and become a buddha, especially with regard to the attainment of buddhahood for icchantikas? An icchantika is a person who not only lacks belief in his or her own buddha nature but who is also antagonistic toward those who teach it. In the second half of the *Nirvana Sutra*, the text clearly states that it is still possible for such a person to attain buddhahood.

In the chapter "Bodhisattva Kashyapa," Sunakshatra Bhikkhu, one of the Buddha's sons in an earlier life when the Buddha was still a bodhisattva, is presented as an icchantika who has severed his roots of goodness. While the World-Honored One admits that his son has indeed done so in the past and continues to do so in the present, he proclaims that no one can prevent a person's roots of goodness from growing in the future. Believing in the possibility of future goodness, the Buddha states that even an icchantika has the potential to achieve buddhahood.

Here the Buddha did not mean that the attainment of buddhahood comes to all spontaneously without concerted effort. Cultivating one's aspiration toward enlightenment and engaging in bodhisattva acts for the well-being of others are the cornerstones to awakening one's buddha nature and giving it full expression. The Buddha urges people to first believe in their buddha nature, take the bodhisattva vow, and train accordingly. Such practice opens the possibility of anyone and everyone attaining buddhahood.

Before he created his nirvana image, Shinjo had gone through a very difficult time as a result of betrayal by a close disciple. Yet this and other painful experiences allowed him to discover the potential found in the teachings of the *Nirvana Sutra*, which declares that all people, even icchantikas, can be awakened and liberated. This experience and others led Shinjo to make the *Nirvana Sutra* the principal doctrinal source for the Shinnyo-en Buddhist tradition.

Shinjo and Tomoji always believed in people. No matter how often they were deceived or betrayed by someone, I remember they continued to believe in the person's potential, talk to them when they had a chance, encourage them, never giving up on them. They always told those who were leaving the sangha: "If you are ever in trouble, come back. A teacher and disciple are connected for life." They cherished the relationships they had with others and treated all those around them with kindness and warmth.

When icchantikas are mentioned in the *Nirvana Sutra*, the term refers to individuals within the Buddhist community. In "Kaundinya," which is the last chapter of the *Nirvana Sutra* as it has come down to us today, the Buddha shifts his focus to address religious practitioners and philosophers from outside the Buddhist community, such as those in the Samkhya and Vedanta schools of the Indian Brahmanism dominant at that time. He also addresses the ascetic-oriented Jain practitioners. The World-Honored One's method of discourse is dialogue. He listens carefully to what the other person has to say, then rationally refutes it, posing his own questions in response. In the process, his counterpart spontaneously gains a new awareness.

In the end, the Buddha's teaching counterparts also awaken to shinnyo, a universal reality. In this way the Buddha preaches paramount emptiness (*parmamartha-shunyata*), which is a positive outlook characterized not by opposition or negation but by harmony. This leads to the idea of "embracement" (Jpn. *shoju*; Skt. *parigraha*) as harmony, and this is upheld in Shinnyo-en as its fundamental orientation toward the world.

Holding Rituals Together and for All People

The World-Honored One made it a rule to convene the sangha several times each month. Those who felt they had somehow created negative karma by giving in to strong impulses like greed and anger had the opportunity to reflect and experience spiritual renewal, allowing them to cast aside old habits or tendencies. This is the origin of rites and rituals in Buddhism. Having a positive vow to engage in wholesome actions is what liberates one from negative karma.

The *Nirvana Sutra* says, "Those who counteract their negative deeds of the past by doing good shall later illuminate the world like a bright moon reappearing from behind the clouds." This teaching expresses the Buddhist belief that goodness gives us the power to break through the darkness and become a light of truth.

Shinjo, Tomoji, and I—as their Dharma successor—have practiced together with many people on our spiritual journey. We have met young people who have lost their parents, who have been betrayed by someone they trusted, or who were in despair at being treated unfairly. We have met people who have lost their family, who have lost their property and all they had in a natural disaster, who have faced severe discrimination, or who could not find hope in the face of a terminal illness. We have tried to do everything we could to welcome these people, offer them spiritual guidance, and encourage them to believe in their innate goodness and their ability to rise above their challenges. Today not only have many of them cultivated spiritual merit (positive karma) themselves, but they are also able to create and extend that merit to benefit others. Having interacted with so many people over the years, I feel that we can say at Shinnyo-en— with conviction—that we all have a buddha nature within us.

In India, many Buddhist archaeological sites survive to this day, including stupas and buddha images with donors' inscriptions. Many carvings contain the set phrase "Let all the merit accrued herein go to my father, mother, and all beings." These spiritual forebears of ours built stupas in the hope that the merit they accrued through their good deeds would benefit their deceased parents and all sentient beings for eternity.

"All sentient beings" here refers to all life in the past, present, and future. The infinity of the "three realms" (past, present, and future) is not delineated by time or space. The limitless scale and worldview of Mahayana Buddhism captures its essence. This Buddhist philosophical perspective bestows upon us various kinds of wisdom throughout the duration of our lives.

Shinnyo-en conducts lantern-floating ceremonies at sites such as a lake at the foot of Mount Fuji and in the ocean around Hawaii as a way of transferring spiritual merit, or the fruit of our good thoughts and actions, to countless others in all realms of existence. When we generate positive karma by acting on the kindness and gratitude that arises from within us at such ceremonies, the merit of those subsequent acts will go around and eventually return to us. For example, when we wake up in the morning, we may offer water at our home altar and place our palms together in *gassho* (placing of one's palms together in prayer, reverence, and gratitude). We may express our care for others by greeting them, serving them a cup of tea, or receiving them warmly. Such acts are all manifestations of the compassion and gratitude that creates positive karma. At such moments, people receive the warmth of the kindness and gratitude that is the experience of buddha nature.

The light of hope for our future lies in the positive karma of transferring the merit we create in our daily situations through our kind thoughts and actions toward others and expanding our individual sphere of goodness infinitely outward. Each of us is unique, and if each person with their individual goodness—their inherent buddha nature—acted in concert with others, we could eventually overcome the difficulties that confront humanity. Of course that will take time. Peace will manifest as we align our intentions with those near to us and find gratitude in our connections to the generations of lives that came before us. Following in the spirit of what Shinjo and Tomoji would have wished, the philanthropic foundations and volunteer organizations established by Shinnyo-en today try to coordinate their efforts to contribute to society in medicine, education, welfare, human rights, environmental conservation, disaster relief, and other fields.

When we all cherish the goodness within ourselves and others, buddha nature is mutually reflected within each of us and shines more brightly. Harmony cannot be handed to us on a plate; it must be created and cultivated. For Shinjo, the *Nirvana Sutra* represents the energy of hope that allows us to do so. It awakens us to the timeless nature of buddhas that we call shinnyo, or buddha nature, latent within our souls, and thus guides us to awaken to our own inherent goodness and spread the good effects of positive karma from one person to the next.

—*Her Holiness Shinso Ito, Spiritual Head of Shinnyo-en*

Note to Readers

Conventions

Most Buddhist terms use either the original Japanese or Sanskrit and are transliterated phonetically (e.g., acharya, dharmakaya, kshanti, nirmanakaya, Shakya). Japanese long vowels have been rendered without the macron, as simply a, e, i, o, u. Japanese personal names appear with given name first.

Citations

To provide an accurate picture of the life experience of Shinjo Ito (1906–1989), we have relied as much as possible on Shinjo's own writing. Shinnyo-en has graciously supplied articles by Shinjo that have appeared in its periodicals, as well as manuscript diaries and notes that Shinjo wrote for himself but never intended to publish. We are very grateful to Shinnyo-en for allowing us to reference these rare primary sources in this biography. Readers will also find quotes from the sources listed below, though in general we do not cite the particular source of any quote.

SHINNYO-EN SOURCES

Shinjo Ito diary entries (unpublished), 1923–1989
Kyoto Gongyo Hen (Chanting Book for General Practitioners), 1948
The Naigai Jiho (Shinnyo-en newsletter), no. 535, 1966
Shinjo Ito. *The Path of Oneness*, 2009
———. *The Light in Each Moment*, 2010
The History of the Shinnyo Path, vol. 1, 2016

OTHER SOURCES

Bunka Jiho, 1962
"Report on Postwar Changes to Religion and Its Relationship to
    Society." Tokyo: The Federation of New Religious Organiza-
    tions of Japan, 1963
Junna Nakada. *Mienai Kokoro wo Miru*, 2007

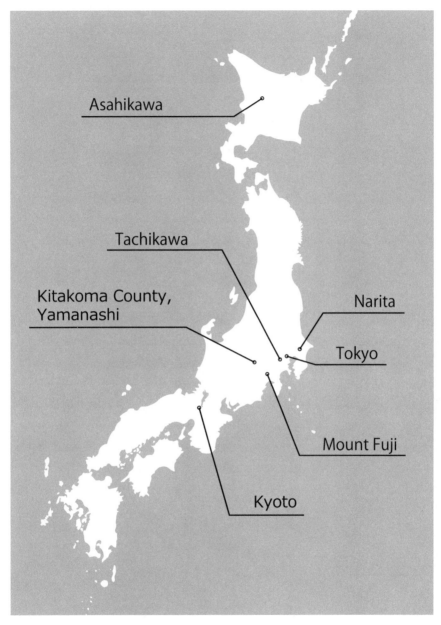

Map of Japan indicating important places in Shinjo Ito's life

I.

FUMIAKI

I.

Boyhood in Yamanashi

A Learned and Spiritual Family

How does a person decide to pursue a religious life? There are numerous roads one can take, of course. Some people become priests because they grow up in a temple and inherit the "family business." Others make the decision as a reaction to a particular trauma, or after encountering continuous problems in their lives, or upon experiencing a moment of enlightenment. But the man who would become Shinjo Ito, the founder of Shinnyo-en, embarked on his religious path in a more circuitous way.

Shinjo's father, Bunjiro, was a devoted practitioner of the Soto school of Japanese Zen. But Shinjo did not grow up in a temple. Nor did he encounter any particular difficulties in his life before becoming a Buddhist. In fact, everything was going well for him both personally and professionally, as Shinjo states in *The Path of Oneness*:[1]

---

1. *The Path of Oneness* was composed by Shinjo in 1957 to show the way to incorporate the teachings of the Buddha into one's life from a threefold perspective: (1) that of doctrine, in particular the teachings based on Shingon esoteric Buddhism and the principles found in the *Nirvana Sutra* (*Mahaparinirvana Sutra*), a seminal text of

Before we enshrined the holy image of Achala I had been working [in the 1930s] as an engineer at the Ishikawajima Aircraft Company for seven years. We were just an ordinary couple with two children enjoying a peaceful family life. (370)

Despite growing up in a religious environment, Shinjo Ito did not dedicate himself fully to Buddhism until he was thirty years old, after he was well into a successful career as an aeronautical engineer. He had a good job and a sound future, and was living a comfortable life with his wife and two children. What inspired him to dedicate himself full time to helping others as a Buddhist monk?

Shinjo's decision and his ultimate role as a Buddhist and spiritual innovator can be traced back to an upbringing rooted in Buddhism and spiritualism and to a well-rounded secular and religious education. He was born with the first name Fumiaki on March 28, 1906, in the village of Akita in Kitakoma county in the Yamanashi Prefecture (today the Nagasaka area in the city of Hokuto). He was the family's second son, the third of seven children, with an older brother and sister, two younger brothers, and two younger sisters. Throughout his life Shinjo maintained a warm feeling toward his hometown. Many people have written eloquently about the spiritual energy of the mountains that loom over Akita from every direction. If you stand with your back to the majestic Yatsugatake Mountains, the southern Japanese Alps soar upward to the right, with Mount Kaikomagatake at their center. To the left is Mount Kinpu, known for the crystal that

Mahayana Buddhism; (2) that which takes into account the way dharma manifests in invisible ways; and (3) that of personal experience.

is mined there. And if you look straight ahead, you will be gazing at the foot of Mount Fuji, one of Japan's three major sacred mountains.

Fumiaki was born into a historically learned family. For generations each head of the Ito household had been well versed in the Chinese classics. It was customary for the head of the family to inherit the name Bunnojo, referring to a "cultured" or "literary" person. That is why the name Fumiaki (文明) begins with the Japanese character 文 that can be read as *fumi* or *bun*, and which refers to the literary arts.

The Itos were a farming clan, prosperous enough to have their own farmhands. Around the time of Fumiaki's birth, his father, Bunjiro, also served as town treasurer. Later he was selected to the village council. Bunjiro was one of the few people of the village who subscribed to a newspaper at this time. Given his background, it is clear

The Yatsugatake mountain range in Yamanashi

Bunjiro was a distinguished man who people trusted. He was also a charitable person. When he served as treasurer many villagers could not afford to pay their taxes. After he died a large box was found in the Ito family storehouse full of receipts for taxes that Bunjiro had paid for others. He had secretly extended his generosity to those around him even though it put a strain on his own family's resources.

Fumiaki was brought up in a multireligious home with elements of traditional Japanese Zen Buddhism, Shintoism, and the Tenrikyo faith. His father walked the path of Zen. Both his father and older brother, Fumishige, served in leadership positions at Seikoji, the local Soto Zen temple, which dates to 1151. Under the guidance of the temple's head priest, Master Chikumei Takahashi, Bunjiro often participated in sessions of *zazen*, or Zen meditation. He was also acquainted with Tokuzan Kumazaki, the head priest of Myokiin, a branch temple of Seikoji. Myokiin, which was established in 1598, may have been founded by ancestors of the Ito family.

Fumiaki's mother, Yoshie, also came from a distinguished family. The Yamamotos are said to descend from Kansuke Yamamoto, the sixteenth-century military strategist for the feudal lord Shingen Takeda. While it is difficult to definitively trace her father's family history, we do know that Yoshie's father was a prominent figure who served as a school principal. His funeral was said to have been the largest in the village's history.

Yoshie was even more committed to her religion than her husband. She was a follower of Tenrikyo, the religion founded by Miki Nakayama, a woman, in the nineteenth century. By the end of the century it had spread throughout Japan. Yoshie regularly attended meetings in the village and often told the young Fumiaki, "When you grow up you will work in the service of something larger than yourself."

After she married Bunjiro, Yoshie continued to cultivate her faith in Tenrikyo under the influence of her mother-in-law, Sono, a devout believer in Tenrikyo. Sono was an educated, cultured person who had a great influence on her grandson Fumiaki. She was born in 1841 and served in the palace until the marriage of the emperor's daughter, Kazunomiya, to Tokugawa Iemochi, the fourteenth shogun, in 1862. In addition to their belief in Tenrikyo, Sono's family had faith in Buddhism and often recited sutras in the home.

Bunjiro seemed to quietly accept his wife's religious activities, but he must have had mixed feelings, since he was a community representative at Seikoji and practiced Zen. Fumiaki later recalled how his father would take him on his lap and talk to him when he was little:

My little one, you are destined for religion. If you wanted to, I think it would be fine if you became a monk. They say that if one person in the family becomes a monk, the merit accrued will reach back seven generations. So if you take to Buddhism, it would be nice if we had a monk in the family.

It is easy to imagine what an impression his father's words would have made on Fumiaki's young mind. Bunjiro may have hoped that if growing up in a family full of faith and devotion were to lead Fumiaki to pursue a religious calling, it would be in pursuit of the Buddhism that he practiced rather than the Tenrikyo faith. Regardless of their personal faiths, both parents expressed the belief that Fumiaki would grow up to be a spiritual person.

Signs and Portents at Birth

Several unusual things happened to Fumiaki when he was an infant. In later years he recounted the events of his own birth:

> You may hear of mysterious phenomena of various types, like a five-colored cloud hovering overhead or a lotus flower opening, for example, that accompanied the births of great spiritual leaders. Nothing like that happened in my case—there were no miracles. If there was anything remarkable about my birth, it is that I was told that I froze to death the moment I was born.

Shinjo was probably being humorous, since freezing to death at birth is hardly an ordinary event. Although he was Yoshie's third child, she suffered severe labor pains and couldn't move on her own immediately after the birth. While her mother-in-law and midwife attended to her, the newborn was apparently left alone. Only after Yoshie recovered somewhat did they realize that the baby was not crying.

The base of the Yatsugatake Mountains are prone to strong winds. On the day Fumiaki was born a seasonal northwesterly wind was blowing down from the mountains and the temperature hovered around freezing. It is unclear how long the other women were attending to his mother, but if the newborn Fumiaki was left alone, it is entirely possible that he would have nearly frozen. The midwife quickly placed the baby in warm water and rubbed him until finally he began to cry.

Apparently Fumiaki had suffered a near-death experience as soon as he came into this world. But the excitement of Fumiaki's first few days wasn't quite over. His father, Bunjiro, was forty-one, an astrolog-ically unlucky age for a man. Because a child born in such an unlucky year was thought to carry bad luck, it was customary in the village of Akita to leave the child with neighbors outside the family home for a period of seven days, after which he would be returned. It was prearranged that one of the town leaders would act as his foster par-ent for the seven days and return him to his parents on the eighth. So although Fumiaki himself said there was nothing extraordinary about his birth, in a sense he was born a second time after a near-death experience, then abandoned and returned home, thus experi-encing, metaphorically speaking, a third death and rebirth.

Unusual birth and abandonment stories figure prominently in the biographies of more than a few Japanese religious figures, in-cluding En no Gyoja (the Ascetic, 634–701), who is considered the founder of the Shugendo tradition of mountain asceticism.[2] Accord-ing to legend, En was born holding a flower in one hand. Amid his newborn cries could be heard the words "Heaven has sent me to save people!" His mother was so terrified, so the story goes, that she took him to the forest and left him there. Yet somehow neither the rain nor dew wetted him, and wild animals protected him. When his mother returned after several days and found him perfectly healthy

---

2. More than three-quarters of the land area in Japan is mountainous and before Buddhism ever arrived, Japan had developed its own religious traditions that flour-ished, finding spirituality in the mountains, as did Shugendo (meaning "the way to spiritual power through discipline"). Shugendo focuses on the development of spiri-tual experience and incorporates various philosophies and ritual systems of East Asia, including pre-Buddhist mountain worship, Shinto, Taoism, and Vajrayana. Over time Shugendo has merged with the Japanese esoteric Buddhism familiar to most people today.

and nourished, she took him back home. Such stories have grown over time into legend. In another legendary biography, Gyoki (668–749), an esteemed monk who was active in helping the poor and spreading Buddhism throughout Japan, was abandoned under a tree until a monk heard him making sounds that resembled the recitation of mantras. He went on to be called a "living bodhisattva."

Although Fumiaki often made light of it over the years, his experiences of birth and abandonment were indeed unusual.

A Fortuitous Connection with Esoteric Buddhism

Fumiaki had at least one other interesting experience as a child. This experience likely made a significant impression on him because it seemed to have cured him of what must have been an embarrassing problem. In 1912 Fumiaki entered Akita Elementary School. His school life was fine except for one small problem: he sometimes still wet his bed at night. It might seem like a minor matter—after all, he was still only six years old. But Fumiaki was terribly troubled by it and his siblings teased him for it. Fumiaki was the only one among his siblings who could not stay overnight with relatives when there was a festival. Fumiaki's mother blamed herself, thinking that the bedwetting was perhaps related to having allowed him to be put outside in the freezing weather when he was a newborn.

During the school year, a woman from the neighborhood known as Granny Shobei came to visit the Ito family. She was also called Granny Kobo because of her well-known devotion to Kukai (also called Kobo Daishi, 774–835), the Japanese Buddhist monk who founded the Shingon, or "True Word," school of Buddhism in Japan.

She would make rounds in the village wearing a white robe and carrying a monk's long crozier that she would pound into the ground as part of her healing rituals.

One day Granny Shobei appeared at the Ito family home, correctly divined that Fumiaki had a problem with bedwetting, and proclaimed that she had received a revelation from Kukai about it. As Fumiaki eavesdropped from behind the sliding paper door, she told Fumiaki's parents that he should take the thumb of his right hand and place it on his chest, move it down to his stomach, then massage his stomach with his thumb seven times in a circle while reciting *Namu Daishi Henjo Kongo* (a mantra expressing reverence for Kukai).

This story seems a bit fantastical, but amazingly after Fumiaki repeated the technique his bedwetting really did stop. Perhaps the event just happened to coincide with the natural end of the problem, but Fumiaki continued to perform this "spell" for some months afterward. In fact, he was quite taken with the *Namu Daishi Henjo Kongo* chant and asked several people what it meant. He learned that *Henjo Kongo* was the name given to Kukai by the Chinese Buddhist master Huiguo, who had initiated Kukai into the esoteric Buddhist tradition. Master Huiguo died shortly after meeting Kukai, but not before instructing him to return to Japan to spread the teachings of esoteric Buddhism there. Thus Kukai is considered the founder of esoteric Buddhism in Japan. Unbeknown to young Fumiaki, this was his first introduction to the Japanese esoteric Buddhist tradition.

The religious name that Huiguo bestowed on Kukai, pronounced "Henjo Kongo" in Japanese, literally means "vajra whose light shines everywhere." The Sanskrit word *vajra* refers to a mythical indestructible object wielded by the gods, and has come to mean "diamond" in common parlance. It is common that disciples of esoteric Buddhism, or the Vajrayana schools of Buddhism (which comes from the Sanskrit term), use the word *vajra* somewhere in their name.

In fact years later, after Fumiaki became a monk, his Buddhist teacher, Egen Saeki, gave him the Dharma name Kongoin Shinjo, which also includes the word *vajra* (*kongo*). When Fumiaki first encountered Kukai's tradition at the age of six, there was no way he could have imagined that he would be initiated at the Daigo school of Shingon Buddhism twenty years later. The experience of being cured by following a method taught by a devout follower of Kukai likely left a lasting impression in his soul.

Love of Art, Science, and Wisdom

Fumiaki was raised in a religious environment, but of course his childhood did not consist only of religion. Like any boy, he played and studied. He got excellent grades, and particularly excelled in science, calligraphy, drawing, and industrial arts. He was good with his hands, and adults were impressed with the countless tiny dolls he created, as well as their even tinier swords and armor. He used ink to dye corn silk to create various wigs for the dolls, including a samurai's topknot. A portrait he drew of his maternal grandfather, Shigeharu Yamamoto, survives to this day. To create the portrait, Fumiaki ordered a set of French conté crayons he had seen in a magazine from a store in Ginza. He then used a group photo of the school graduation ceremony to draw the picture using a magnifying glass. The drawing, which is extremely detailed even down to the hair on his grandfather's head, looks like a photograph. It won a prize at an exhibition in Yamanashi Prefecture.

Fumiaki was devoted to his studies and throughout the year was often seen jotting down notes about what he was reading. He was already an avid reader, a habit that continued throughout his life, and seems to have preferred nonfiction books in the humanities. Even after he became an accomplished monk and priest, he continued to study sutras and other religious source materials.

In February 1917, when Fumiaki was ten, an airplane flew over Yamanashi. It caused an aeronautical craze among the local children.

The portrait that Fumiaki drew of his grandfather

The event made a lasting impression on Fumiaki. He showed talent in this regard, making an elaborate model airplane and turning it into a mechanical flying toy. To make it lighter so it could fly, he used a bamboo chopstick as a propeller shaft, bent wire into the shape of wings, and covered the plane with Japanese paper. He then carved a propeller from bamboo, warmed it over a candle flame, twisted it, and fine-tuned it with a carving knife.

School photo of fourteen-year-old Fumiaki (*center*)

These episodes are not surprising, considering Fumiaki's later career as an aeronautical engineer. But his training in the Byozeisho under the guidance of his father beginning in 1918, the year he entered Akita Junior High School, had an even greater influence on his future. The Byozeisho is a method of spiritual discernment, related to the *I Ching* (Chinese *Yijing*, meaning the "Book of Changes"), and had been passed down orally in the Ito family for generations. Fumiaki received teachings in this divining method from his father over the course of several years, usually when they were alone together in the fields weeding or performing other farming chores.

The *I Ching* originated in ancient China. It first reached Japan in the sixth century, where it began to develop a uniquely Japanese flavor. The discipline didn't spread widely there until the seventeenth century. By many accounts, Shingen Takeda (1521–73), the military commander of what is now Yamanashi Prefecture and one of the top military leaders during the Warring States period (c. 1467–c. 1600), planned his military maneuvers using this method, which helped to popularize various forms of divination. During the rule of the Tokugawa Shogunate from 1603 until 1868, more than a thousand books were written on the *I Ching*. Astoundingly, this number is about the same as the number of books on the topic written in China, a country with a population fifteen times the size of Japan's population.

One strand of the *I Ching* tradition was passed down from one generation to the next within the Ito family. It was originally only transmitted orally, but in his later years Shinjo spent time selecting certain Chinese characters with which to write the term *Byozeisho*. Up to then, its written form had not been established. Shinjo recalled that by listening to his father's lectures, "at some point the concepts in the study

of spiritual discernment got through my head and I had almost completely mastered the subject's difficult specialized vocabulary." Bunjiro
regularly offered consultations to villagers based on the Byozeisho, but
always told Fumiaki, "This is a private oral transmission and it must
never be used for profit."

After graduating from Akita Junior High School in March
1920, Fumiaki continued for another year studying advanced sup-
plementary coursework at Akita Agricultural High School. In May
1921, at the age of fifteen, he became an apprentice at a metal uten-
sil store managed by an acquaintance of his father's in Asahikawa,
Hokkaido—over 1,126 kilometers away from his hometown. Going
to Hokkaido in those days was an arduous journey. Fumiaki first

Fumiaki at the age of eighteen

had to board a train on the Chuo Line for Tokyo, then transfer to the Tohoku Main Line and change trains several times to get to the northernmost part of the Honshu island. Then he had to take the Seikan ferry across the Tsugaru Strait to the island of Hokkaido. There he took a train for another ten hours across the vast plains of Hokkaido before finally reaching Asahikawa.

Two months after Fumiaki arrived in Asahikawa, his father passed away at the age of fifty-four from what is thought to have been acute peritonitis. No photographs of Bunjiro survive. But when Shinjo was fifty-two he sculpted a relief of his father's face as he remembered it. By then Shinjo was a father himself several times over. Perhaps he created the image not only out of love for his father

A relief sculpture of Bunjiro Ito made by Shinjo in 1958

but also to convey a sense of this man who had to leave six children behind when he passed away.

Given the distance and difficulty of the journey, Fumiaki was not able to get home in time for his father's funeral. In fact, he did not return until June of the following year.

Upon returning home Fumiaki found his mother almost unrecognizable, blackened by the dirt of hard work on the farm and tanned by the scorching sun. He later wrote:

> She was a widow in her forties, and it was not easy with six children. Of course, I helped with the farm work, and when I sat down on a ridge to rest I would always think of my father.

Yoshie's faith in Tenrikyo became even stronger after her husband's death. A new Tenrikyo branch had just been established near Nagasaka station, and Yoshie was listed as one of its founders. From the moment of his return, Fumiaki's days were filled with fieldwork and services at the Tenrikyo church. Although he never formally considered himself a practitioner of the Tenrikyo faith, he did express his admiration for the way Tenrikyo members devoted themselves totally to the act of service.

Even at the young age of sixteen Fumiaki knew he would not be content living as a farm worker covered in dirt. "I wanted to study," he recalled years later. "I wanted to go to Tokyo. And even if I had to work my way through school, I wanted to study at a technical school. This feeling grew only stronger and stronger." So in 1923, at the age of seventeen, Fumiaki persuaded his mother to let him move to Tokyo.

2

A Young Man in Tokyo

Fascination with Technology and a
Growing Spiritual Capacity

One of Fumiaki's intentions was to study English. But two of his uncles who lived in Tokyo, younger brothers of both his mother and father, opposed that plan. He struck out on his own and went to work for the Central Telegraph Office.[3] Fumiaki did not give up on the idea of pursuing his studies, however. The following year, in April 1924, he enrolled at the Seisoku English School (now called Seisoku Gakuen) while continuing to work at the telegraph office. After graduating at the age of nineteen, he took a second job at Taiseido, a shop that sold photography supplies in the Kanda Nishikicho district of Tokyo.

The same year, the Tokyo Broadcasting Bureau made its first radio broadcast, an event that triggered a radio boom throughout Japan. In those days, a typical domestic model was a crystal radio that picked up a lot of static and was audible only when the listener's ear was pressed tightly against the receiver. The quality of foreign

---

3. Now the Nippon Telegraph and Telephone Corporation, or NTT.

radios, especially the vacuum-tube models produced by the American manufacturer Crosley, was much higher. Fumiaki got hold of a radio-wiring diagram from the United States, and using his English and engineering skills, he succeeded in putting together a radio that quickly became a bestseller for Taiseido.

Also during this time Fumiaki began studying photography with Toragoro Ariga, a prominent portrait photographer who had returned from studying in Germany. At the time, photography was an advanced technology, not yet easily accessible to the general public. A German-made Leica camera was so expensive that people would joke, "Should I buy a Leica or a house?" So the young Fumiaki's curiosity must have indeed been strong to get involved in the field.

Young Fumiaki in 1924

In December 1926 Emperor Taisho passed away, marking the end of the Taisho era (1912–26) and the beginning of the Showa era (1926–89) under the reign of Emperor Hirohito. Fumiaki was twenty years old.

Fumiaki's older brother, Fumishige, recounts an interesting episode from around this time. Because he was the eldest son, Fumishige succeeded their father as head of the Ito household. He seems to have had an outspoken personality and inspired trust in people, even serving as the head of the town council.

Fumiaki is my younger brother. Ambitious from an early age, he went to Tokyo and worked his way through school. When Fumiaki was about nineteen, an uncle of ours, about seventy years old at the time, was living a lonely life after his wife died and his son moved abroad. When he heard that Fumiaki was coming to visit from Tokyo, he said, "I want to hear what interesting things he has to say." He was very weak but he walked to the Ito ancestral home, and as he was listening to Fumiaki he collapsed, falling forward with his face in Fumiaki's lap.

If it had been me, I probably would have made a big fuss and maybe even have fled in fright. But when I rushed over Fumiaki was sitting calmly with our uncle's head still in his lap. I still remember that moment, Fumiaki looking as big as a mountain, talking soothingly to our uncle. "Uncle," he said, "it's good that you came home to die." Fumiaki stayed like that, holding our uncle in his lap until it was time to take his body back to his own house.

Nineteen is still young. A person at that age, unless he has a lot of experience, probably does not yet understand much about life and death. As Fumiaki's brother Fumishige recounts, most teenagers would probably have panicked if a man fell into their arms and stopped breathing. But Fumiaki reacted calmly and even spoke warmly to his uncle. We can already glimpse the spiritual core that would sustain Fumiaki through the personal tragedies that lay ahead and inspire him to become a spiritual leader.

At the time, however, Fumiaki himself was not yet sure which path he was going to follow. He was interested in several cutting-edge subjects, including learning the English language, radio, and photography, and he displayed talent in all of them. It seemed as if he were heading toward a career in a technological field.

Military Man and Aircraft Engineer

In 1927 Fumiaki's professional path was interrupted when he was drafted into the Japanese military. On January 10 he was assigned to the Air Force Division's Fifth Regiment in the Imperial Army. He followed the custom of the time by entrusting part of the money he had earned at Taiseido to his mother for a sendoff before his induction. In *The Light in Each Moment* Shinjo reminisces:

> As the autumn of that first year waned, I was urged to apply for a noncommissioned officer position to "better serve my country." I loved airplanes, but I also knew unequivocally that I was not cut out for a military career and I made my refusal quite clear. I wanted only to learn more about photography, which I liked very much, and to serve my two-year tour of duty. Nevertheless, at the end of January 1928 I was unexpectedly promoted to Airman First Class with orders to seek promotion to noncommissioned officer rank, and was assigned to the machinery and parts-supply section.

The Fifth Air Force Regiment was part of the Imperial Guard, under the direct command of the emperor. Only men with the best references, health, and scholastic records were eligible for service. As Airman First Class, Fumiaki was put in charge of recording the flight times of the officers. As part of his responsibilities, he had the opportunity to fulfill a long-held childhood dream of riding in an airplane. Aircraft engineering technology was progressing rapidly, and Fumiaki often accompanied senior officers on their missions in the modern Salmson model, a two-seater biplane constructed mostly of wood and silk.

Fumiaki at the time of serving in the Fifth Air Force Regiment

In those days, pilots returning to land at the airfield in Tachikawa used Suwa woods, with its huge, dense pine trees, as a landmark. As he flew over them, Fumiaki must have frequently observed the future location of Shinnyo-en's temple site, not knowing of course that in ten years' time, right next to these woods, he would establish the first Shinnyo-en temple. Today that location is headquarters of the Shinnyo-en sangha.

After attending a large-scale military review held for the emperor on December 2, 1928, Fumiaki was released from military service and returned to his hometown. A crowd of neighbors and members of the local veterans' association came out to the station to welcome him. One of the well-wishers offered him a ride on his horse, so he leisurely returned home on horseback.

Almost immediately Fumiaki was offered a job as an aeronautical engineer with the Ishikawajima Aircraft Company (later Ishikawajima Aircraft Company Limited) in Tsukishima, Tokyo. Because of his experience in the military, he was appointed as section leader to oversee the work of several dozen subordinates. His department became responsible for designing and producing aerial photographic devices, dashboards, and other parts that could be considered the heart or brains of the airplane, and for coordinating production with other departments.

Following the First World War, the Japanese economy had experienced a major downturn sparked by several events, including the Great Kanto Earthquake of 1923, a domestic financial crisis in 1927, and the global economic depression triggered by the 1929 Wall Street crash in the United States. At the same time, reactionary elements led by the Japanese military began advocating for the invasion of foreign countries as the solution to political and economic woes at home.

In 1931, a staged event engineered by rogue Japanese military personnel was used as a pretext for the Japanese invasion of northeastern

China. This became known as the Manchurian Incident. It plunged Japan into the period referred to as the Fifteen-Year War, primarily between Japan and China. Since it was marked by the prominence of military affairs, Fumiaki's field of aeronautical engineering became an extremely important national priority. Professionally he began to thrive, and he was soon earning a monthly salary of just over 200 yen, twice as much as a Tokyo government section chief. Naojiro Ishizuka, one of Fumiaki's senior colleagues at the time, recalls the first week when both he and Fumiaki lived in Tsukishima:

> In the early days at Tsukishima the company wasn't so busy. We had no overnight duties or overtime, and we finished work fairly early each day. I have so many fond memories of that time. In the evenings, we'd have a 12-sen dinner and sometimes take a leisurely walk to Ginza.[4] We didn't have any spare cash, so all we could do was walk around, go back to our lodgings, and sleep. It was hardly an extravagant lifestyle, but we enjoyed it. What I can't forget is hearing Fumiaki sing. One day we were with another colleague and we started singing. When it was Fumiaki's turn, he sang *The Song of the Volga Boatmen* in English. It was truly beautiful.

Practitioner of the Byozeisho

During these years, Fumiaki never stopped practicing the *I Ching* in the form of the Byozeisho. He had been strongly warned by his father

---

4. Ginza was (and remains today) one of the most fashionable, upscale shopping districts in Tokyo. Then as now, people enjoy taking leisurely strolls along its long, wide avenues.

never to use this form of spiritual discernment for personal gain, and he followed that advice. But he did sometimes use it to advise friends and colleagues.

In addition to being busy with his work at Ishikawajima Aircraft, Fumiaki also began to study at the Dai Nihon Ekisen Doshikai (Japanese Divination Society) in Koishikawa, Tokyo. He attended evening lectures on both divination and phrenology[5] by the sixth-generation master Sekiryushi. Later, Fumiaki became certified as a master himself. No doubt he hoped that by systematically learning divination he could deepen his understanding of the Byozeisho that his father had transmitted to him.

The *I Ching* is based on eight trigrams—eight different combinations of solid and broken lines that serve as the basis for interpreting all phenomena. The Japanese often say, "Both the accurate and inaccurate are expressions of the eight trigrams"—in other words, it is understood that predictions may or may not come true. But Fumiaki's counsel based on the Byozeisho had a reputation for accuracy. Each day when he arrived home from work there was typically a small group of people waiting to consult with him. They asked him all kinds of questions related to their work and family, even what to name their children. Fumiaki's use of the Byozeisho was so trusted that some of his military commanders began asking his advice.

"Designing aircraft equipment is extremely delicate work," Fumiaki once reminisced. "Absolutely no mistakes are permitted. A finished part may look simple but its design is complex. If something

---

5. Phrenology is a now-debunked science that studied the structure of the skull to determine a person's character and mental capacity.

From around 1930 onward, Fumiaki helped people
with the Byozeisho divination.

goes wrong, it is very difficult to locate the source of the malfunction.
Many times, the Byozeisho helped me discover the mistake."

Fumiaki was becoming well known for his abilities. Naojiro
Ishizuka recalls the time he went to have his fortune read in Ikebu-
kuro, where fortunetellers lined the street. He told the fortuneteller
about Fumiaki and his divination skills, and the man replied, seemingly startled at hearing Fumiaki's name, "So you know Mr. Ito of
Tachikawa? Well, in that case, I can't take any money from you." It
seems that Fumiaki's name was already quite celebrated in this circle.

Seikichi Igarashi, another of Fumiaki's coworkers at Ishikawajima Aircraft, tells another story about these years:

I joined the company in November 1928 and Fumiaki joined in January of the following year. When the factory relocated from Tsukishima to Tachikawa, Fumiaki became our group leader. As perhaps is fitting for someone who would later become a spiritual leader, Fumiaki seemed unique from the very beginning. Immediately I noticed that he had a very different perspective compared to his peers. Many military veterans in the company were arrogant. They threw their weight around, barked orders, and openly displayed favoritism. Fumiaki was never like that. He treated everyone equally and paid a great deal of attention to those around him. His leadership also earned the trust of his superiors. I became determined to follow his lead.

While excelling as an engineer, Fumiaki was also highly knowledgeable in the area of spiritual discernment. He gave advice not only on personal problems but also on difficult issues related to work. Once he read my palm and told me, "It seems important for you to engage in some type of spiritual practice. Doing so will open up a brighter future for you." Those words are still etched in my memory.

Husband and Father

It wasn't unusual in early twentieth-century Japan, particularly outside of major cities, for a bride and groom not to meet in person until their wedding day. Fumiaki's marriage to Tomoji Uchida on April 27, 1932, was arranged by his mother and other relatives.

"I promise not to complain about your choice," he told his mother, "but I have just one condition: I'd like to marry someone who has persevered despite difficulties in her life."

Photos of Fumiaki and Tomoji taken around the time of their wedding

Tomoji certainly fit that description. Her childhood in a small village about 5 kilometers northeast of Fumiaki's village of Akita had not been a carefree one. She lost her father when she was three, and four years later her mother remarried and left Tomoji and her younger sister in their grandmother's care. Later she lost her sister to illness, as she recalled years later:

My sister caught a bad case of fever, and as she died, she called out, "Mother! Mother!" Our mother arrived afterward and called out my sister's name as she cried. I wanted to say, "It's no use calling for her now when she's not here anymore. You are the one who has made us so unhappy. Why did you leave us?" At the time, I still carried so much resentment toward my mother for what had happened.

It took Tomoji many years to feel differently about her mother, as she later wrote:

> When I did the laundry at the river, I tried to imagine my feelings toward my mother be purified by the flow of the clean water. But no matter how much I wanted that to happen, the bitterness remained. Then after I married Shinjo and started to walk a spiritual path, I began to understand the concept of equanimity, of treating both friend and foe equally. My bitter feelings started to fade and at last I could forgive my mother.

Tomoji was raised by her grandmother, Kin Uchida, who became her most important influence. Kin was a devotee of Buddhist traditions centered on the *Lotus Sutra*. She started working in a Buddhist mission in Yokohama in 1868 and developed spiritual abilities to perform faith healings upon request. Influenced by her grandmother, Tomoji came to feel close to two figures of awakening that appear in the *Lotus Sutra*, Yakushi[6] and Kannon.[7] In these years it was very unusual for girls to advance past elementary school unless they were from well-to-do families. Nevertheless, Tomoji attended higher elementary school (today's middle school or junior high), walking each day more than 1.5 kilometers up a steep mountain path in wooden

---

6. In Sanskrit, *Bhaishajyaguru*; in English, the "Medicine Buddha."

7. In Sanskrit, *Avalokiteshvara*, probably the best known of all the archetypal bodhisattvas and a figure widely venerated throughout East Asia. She embodies the loving-kindness and compassion of all buddhas, expressed through a willingness to extend boundless help to all beings who suffer. Representatives of Avalokiteshvara are found in both male and female form; however, in China (known as *Kuan Yin*) and in Japan (as *Kannon*) Avalokiteshvara is revered as the "Mother of All Humanity" and is most commonly feminine.

clogs. In winter the path would frequently disappear under deep snow, making the trip difficult. She was the only girl from her village to attend junior high school, and she graduated in two years. In September 1930, after her grandmother passed away and her brother married, she moved to the city of Kofu and attended a kimono-making school.

Fumiaki was twenty-six and Tomoji twenty when they married. Like Fumiaki, Tomoji was born in Kitakoma county in the prefecture of Yamanashi. Their grandmothers were sisters, which meant Fumiaki's mother and Tomoji's father were cousins. Fumiaki and Tomoji were therefore second cousins, which was not unusual for newlyweds at that time.

Tomoji immediately began to have an influence on Fumiaki's spiritual life. In the early years of their marriage, for example, she began to share her interest in Kannon. Soon, each morning and evening, they were together reciting from the part of the *Lotus Sutra* dedicated to the bodhisattva Kannon. But Fumiaki was clearly open to other religious ideas, too. He even began to frequent the Holiness Church, a Protestant community in Shinjuku where his older sister, Yoshiko, was a member.

In 1933 their first child, a daughter, was born. Shortly afterward, to be closer to Fumiaki's work, the family moved to Tachikawa. It was there in the following year that their son Chibun was born.

"In personal terms, I think this was the happiest I have ever been," Tomoji later reminisced. "As the second son, Shinjo had no inheritance. And without parents, I had no bridal dowry, so we began our lives together with hardly any material possessions of our own. We began, as the Japanese say, with just two pairs of chopsticks. Taking care of the children kept us busy, but we were content in the private space of our family life."

The young Ito family at Inokashira Park in 1935

Prior to its rapid development in the early twentieth century, the city of Tachikawa in the western metropolitan area of Tokyo was a small, quiet village. Mulberry fields were everywhere, and the locals raised silkworms as the main cottage industry. The village began shifting toward modernization in 1889 with the opening of the Kobu Railway (the present-day Chuo Line of East Japan Railways). In 1922 a military airport was built, and the village grew into a military town that became known as the "city of airplanes."

In April 1928, after the Ishikawajima Aircraft Company was chosen as the official manufacturer for the Japanese Imperial Army's aerial division, the company decided to relocate from the Tsukishima district of Tokyo and construct a new factory in Tachikawa. The opening of a commercial airport the following year in 1929 brought prominent international aviators, along with other foreign and domestic travelers. When Fumiaki first set foot in Tachikawa, the township was already transforming from a sleepy village into a military metropolis.

3.

Settling Down

Diviner, Photographer, and Buddhist

On July 29, 1934, Fumiaki and Tomoji's son Chibun was born, and in October the family moved to the Nanko-cho area of Tachikawa. By this time Japan was on a war footing and Fumiaki's company was increasing production almost daily. Although he was busy at work, he continued to study and use the Byozeisho to help others. Every day, people came to seek his counsel and guidance. His divination sessions would often extend far into the night.

The residential area on the south side of Tachikawa railway station, where the Ito family lived from 1934 to 1938. Photo courtesy of the Tachikawa City Historical Folk Museum.

In 1935 Kuniko Nakamura became Fumiaki and Tomoji's neighbor. Years later she shared her recollections of those days:

> My father, a policeman, transferred to Tachikawa and we moved into a
> house just two doors from Fumiaki and Tomoji's home. My father would
> patrol the neighborhood each night. After ten o'clock, lights in the homes
> and shopping districts generally went out, since hardly anyone engaged in
> evening entertainment in those days. At first he thought it very strange that
> the Itos' house was often brightly lit until very late, and that they seemed to
> have many visitors. However, soon he heard from the townsfolk that Mr.
> Ito was a company worker by day, but helped people at night using a highly
> accurate divinatory practice. So even before his sangha was established,
> Fumiaki was helping people through the Byozeisho.

One day the Byozeisho revealed to Fumiaki that within the next
week if great care was not taken, a fire could break out in the quadrant of his office located to the northeast of the general affairs section. He immediately warned the people in that department and
insisted that they make doubly sure they had fire-fighting equipment
ready. Within a week a fire did break out in the place where he had
foreseen, but because they were prepared with the necessary equipment, a disaster was averted.

After that incident, Fumiaki's company asked him to take on the
specialized work of solving, foreseeing, and preventing problems
using the Byozeisho. But his father had strongly advised him against
practicing it for personal gain or profit, so he declined.

Some readers may wonder whether any of these claims about
the use of divination tools are true. Can the Byozeisho or *I Ching*

really predict the future? "Of course," one might think, "rational people do not rely on divination." No doubt Fumiaki himself must have considered this. His study of English, his work building radios, and his career as an aeronautical engineer all demonstrate that he was a rational person. His work colleagues were also engineers in an industry that requires scientific precision, so naturally they were not likely to believe in something that falls outside of the realm of scientifically rational. To us nowadays, this might seem like a paradox, but the fact was that Fumiaki's practice of the Byozeisho inspired the confidence of people from all walks of life.

Even now, in the twenty-first century, as our cell phones can serve as our personal computer and countless manmade satellites orbit the earth, people continue to believe in what cannot be explained by science. Magazines still publish horoscopes based on astrology and other practices, and Japanese television regularly broadcasts programs on psychic and occult phenomena. Their audiences may not necessarily believe in phenomena like spirits or life after death, but people often encounter the unexplainable. Fumiaki believed, as do many others, that some things in this world cannot be explained through common sense or modern reason alone.

As Fumiaki was rising through the ranks of his profession as a valued engineer, he was also being noticed as an accomplished photographer. In 1934 he was awarded first prize in a photographic competition sponsored by the Yomiuri newspaper. The following year he won second prize in an exhibition sponsored by the Tama Gakokai Association. That same year a photograph by Fumiaki was published on the opening page of the April issue of the monthly publication *Gendai* (Today) accompanying a poem called "Hikari" (Light) by

Photos by Fumiaki believed to have been taken in his late twenties

Saisei Muro. Muro had gained prominence in 1918 with the publication of two popular books of poetry,[8] and with the release the following year of two novels,[9] confirmed his status as an important writer. The publication of a photograph beside a poem by such an established writer was surely a coup for an amateur photographer like Fumiaki, and evidence of his growing skill.

Not many of Fumiaki's photographs survive, but the ones that do are full of vivid contrasts and deep shades that weave together light and shadow. Even now they are beautiful works, and they suggest that if Fumiaki had not chosen to become an aeronautical engineer, perhaps he would have made a career in photography. Ultimately, of course, he chose neither of those paths.

These were busy years for Fumiaki and Tomoji, particularly since Fumiaki had a growing community of people who sought his guidance based on his expertise in the Byozeisho. At first they were just friends and acquaintances, but gradually those people began to invite others and their numbers increased. Every evening a group of people continued to wait for Fumiaki when he came home, seeking his advice. Fumiaki began to realize that while he could use the Byozeisho to help people make life decisions, it would take more than that to help them deal with the anxiety and struggles that are inevitable in life. He realized that answers to deeper questions were what he had been looking for in his life thus far. As he explains in *The Light in Each Moment*:

> Looking back, I realize that I had become familiar with a number of teachings and schools of thought. I learned about Zen Buddhism from my father

---

8. *Ai no shishu* (Poems of Love) and *Jojo shokyokushu* (Lyrical Pieces).
9. *Yonen jidai* (My Childhood) and *Sei ni mezameru koro* (As I Was Awakened to Sex).

and was guided to the Tenrikyo faith through my mother. During my time in the military I even became acquainted with physiognomy.[10] I developed a devotion to Bodhisattva Kannon from Tomoji, and I learned about Christianity from my sister. A friend at work taught me about Pure Land Buddhism, and the wife of another friend introduced me to the teachings of the *Lotus Sutra*. It was as though some mysterious hand was guiding me to study and experience all these beliefs.

All this study culminated with Fumiaki's discovery of Shingon esoteric Buddhism, thanks to Shuko Obori, a Shingon priest who had heard about Fumiaki's work with the Byozeisho. Obori asked Fumiaki to instruct him in this spiritual discernment practice. In return, he offered to teach Fumiaki everything he knew about esoteric Buddhism, and soon Fumiaki was devoting many hours to serious study of the Shingon teachings.

By offering the Byozeisho consultations to people without charge, even when he was extremely busy with work and family, Fumiaki already showed an eagerness to put the interests of other people before his own. It should come as no surprise, then, that he was eventually drawn to a kind of Buddhism that places special emphasis on the path of becoming a "larger vehicle" that can journey toward awakening by taking others along as well.

---

10. The art of discovering temperament and character from outward appearance, especially the face. From the Greek *physis*, meaning "nature," and *gnomon*, meaning "judge" or "interpreter."

Finding Achala

It is common for serious practitioners of Buddhism to bring a buddha figure into their home as a personal symbol of their practice. In Fumiaki's case, Achala (Jpn. Fudo) was a natural choice. Fumiaki initially thought of enshrining a statue of Kannon, but he was intrigued by the beautiful hanging scroll of Achala that Obori displayed in his own small shrine. Obori was a Shingon practitioner, and within that tradition Achala is one of the main figures of an awakened, deep state of concentration.

Painting of Achala created by Shinjo in 1947

It was during the early Heian period (794–1185) that Kukai established Shingon esoteric Buddhism in Japan and brought texts and images of Achala to Japan. The name Achala, or Achalanatha (Jpn. Fudo-o), means "unwavering one." Achala is the most commonly venerated of all the vidyarajas, or "illumination lords"—fierce-looking buddha figures with wrathful expressions.[11] Like tathagatas and bodhisattvas, vidyarajas are important archetypes in Buddhist cosmology. In general, they personify our ability to overcome hindrances and obstacles with firm resolve; in particular, they embody one aspect of buddhahood, that of steadfast, unshakable resolve grounded in loving-kindness. Achala's frightening appearance is assumed to ward off only negativity and protect against bad behavior, like a stern father who disciplines a child out of love. Several rituals are associated with Achala, including the *homa* fire ritual.[12]

Fumiaki began searching for his own statue of Achala but could not find one that satisfied him. Finally, he heard about a Buddhist sculptor named Odo Nakamaru. Master Nakamaru was known for having sculpted many different images of vidyarajas. These included many of Achala, for which he used his family's historic statue as a model.

In the late summer of 1935, Fumiaki visited the sculptor at his home studio in the Kagurazaka neighborhood of Tokyo. The first statue he saw was actually not Master Nakamaru's creation, but the one he used as a model. It was of a seated Achala, said to have been sculpted by Unkei, the famous Buddhist sculptor of the early Kama-

---

11. In Shingon esoteric Buddhism the "five wisdom kings, or illumination lords," in addition to Achala, include Gozanze (Skt. Trailokya-vijaya-raja), Gundari (Skt. Kundali), Daiitoku (Skt. Yamantaka), and Kongoyasha (Skt. Vajrayaksha).
12. Discussed in chapter 5, the section "Homa: The Ritual at the Heart of Practice."

kura period (1185–1333). Unkei displayed his gifts from a young age and continued to create buddha images until his death at about seventy years old. Among his most celebrated works are the two Nio guardians[13] sculpted in 1203 that protect the Great South Gate of the Todaiji monastic complex in Nara.

The warlord Tokimasa Hojo commissioned Unkei to sculpt Buddhist statues for Ganjojuin, a temple in the town of Nirayama. Master Nakamaru's Achala figure, which had been passed down in his family, was said to have been created especially for Tokimasa Hojo's personal use.

The Achala statue greatly impressed Fumiaki. He was particularly struck by its distinguished facial expressions. Usually Achala is sculpted with "heaven-and-earth eyes"—the right eye staring up toward heaven and the left staring down toward earth. But this figure bore clear eyes that looked straight ahead with a steady gaze.

Fumiaki was also impressed with Master and Mrs. Nakamaru. In his journal, Fumiaki describes Mrs. Nakamaru as "a cheerful middle-aged woman, probably older than I was. To me she seemed like the genteel lady of a well-to-do manor rather than a simple shop owner's wife."

As for the sculptor, Fumiaki described him as resembling Jubei, a character from the novella *Five-Storied Pagoda*,[14] by Rohan Koda.

---

13. Nio guardians are the two muscular, wrathful protectors of the Buddha that stand at the entrance to Buddhist temples across Asia. They are manifestations of Bodhisattva Vajrapani, protector and guide of the Buddha, who came to symbolize his power. According to Japanese tradition, the Nio guardians traveled with the historical Buddha to protect him.

14. *The Five-Storied Pagoda*, one of Koda's best-known stories, tells of Jubei, a poor apprenticed workman who dares to dream of building a famous temple's new five-storied pagoda. He grows so bold as to compete with his own master.

"He was a stout, quiet man who spoke with frequent pauses," Fumiaki later wrote. "He seemed to have the character of a craftsman, but not just any craftsman, a master craftsman and true artist" (*The History of the Shinnyo Path*, 84). Although at the time Fumiaki wasn't aware of its significance, he also noted that Master Nakamaru shaved his head every three days.

Most important, however, Fumiaki was smitten with the statue of Achala, and he asked for a new image to be made for him, one modeled on that Achala. Master Nakamaru agreed and promised to have it ready in three months.

Then events took a mysterious turn. Master Nakamaru had been sculpting Buddhist statues for many years, specializing in images of the vidyarajas, including Achala. However, for some reason he was not able to make the image that Fumiaki had commissioned. When Fumiaki returned three months later, the master made him an unexpected proposal: "I'm sorry. I cannot sculpt the image of Achala you requested. He would not let me. This is the first time such a thing has happened in my experience, but I believe this buddha figure wants to go home with you."

The statue was an important historical image attributed to one of its era's most revered Buddhist sculptors, Unkei. He is said to have performed three prostrations of devotion with every strike of his chisel. Nevertheless, much to Fumiaki's surprise, Master Nakamaru offered Fumiaki the statue for a donation of only 300 yen, about 1.5 times Fumiaki's monthly salary at the time. Fumiaki later recalled the day he enshrined the Achala statue in his home with deep emotion, remembering it "as though it was yesterday."

Odo Nakamaru (*far right*)

Welcoming Achala into His Home

On December 28, 1935, Fumiaki rose at 4:30 a.m., full of excitement. He first underwent cold water ablutions to purify himself, reciting a verse for purification that his grandmother had taught him as a boy. Fumiaki used the pure, icy water from a 70-liter barrel stored outside in the midst of winter, scooping it out repeatedly and pouring it on himself. After putting on the clean clothes Tomoji had prepared for him, he went to the small shrine he had dedicated to the four sages related to the Byozeisho—Fu Xi, King Wen of the Zhou, the Duke of Zhou, and Confucius—and performed prostrations. He then set out for the Nakamaru residence about two hours away by car.

Years later Fumiaki recalled his visit to the home of Master and Mrs. Nakamaru:

I was accompanied by young Kiichi Shimura, who hailed from the same province of Yamanashi as myself and acted as a representative of my supporters.[15] He was in high spirits and very excited about bringing the image of Achala back to Tachikawa. The snow, which had been falling incessantly since the previous day, continued to come down heavily. Azuma Taxi had been booked in advance to pick us up at 8:00 a.m., and my wife came out to see us off when the taxi arrived five minutes early.

We drove along the road that leads to the southern entrance of the railway station, down a side street by Fuchu Second Middle School, and turned onto the Koshu Highway. By then the snow was coming down thick and fast, and by the time the car passed Yaho Shrine large flakes had appeared that reduced visibility.

It took them almost three hours to get to the Nakamaru residence. Upon their arrival, Mrs. Nakamaru came out to welcome them. Fumiaki first went to the Achala image to pay his respects.

At that moment, the words of Mrs. Nakamaru came back to him. "By using this Achala as a model," she had told him, "my husband studied statues of fierce-looking buddhas and became enthusiastic about carving them himself. Known to have been created by Unkei, such a distinguished sculptor, we want it to be enshrined by the appropriate person."

---

15. Fumiaki's group of supporters at the time were mostly associated with him through the Ishikawajima Aircraft Company and his practice of the Byozeisho.

Whether or not the stories about the statue were true, there was no doubt that it was a very old, valuable Buddhist work of art worth considerably more than 300 yen. What's more, Odo Nakamaru had gained a reputation as a master Buddhist sculptor who specialized in illumination lord statues, and this was an important model from which he fashioned Buddhist images.

Why was it that Master Nakamaru could not make an image of Achala, and why was he willing to part with such an important family heirloom, particularly for such a modest price? Various thoughts came rushing to Fumiaki's mind. To clear his mind he performed the *kuji* procedure, reciting *Rin pyou tou sha kai chin retsu zai zen*—"Celestial soldiers descend and arrange yourselves in front of me!" *Kuji* simply means "nine syllables," and refers to the chant for the procedure.

Fumiaki finally felt convinced: something beyond human ken was working to make him the custodian of that Achala statue.

Later Fumiaki also described a hanging scroll to the right of Achala by an unknown artist that bore the inscription "The moonlight on the peak of Mount Koya, gazed upon by countless generations." To the left was a statue of Shakyamuni at the time of his birth. Every tiny detail of that day was etched into Fumiaki's memory, because the day he received the Achala statue was the point at which his path turned decisively toward full-time dedication to Buddhism.

Along with the Achala statue, Master Nakamaru also gave Fumiaki a set of old mantras—three volumes dated 1693. The name of a high-ranking Tendai Buddhist monk, who had once possibly owned the Achala statue, was written on the back of these texts. As he listened to Master Nakamaru explain the history of the Achala image, Fumiaki noted the openness with which he spoke of various faith traditions other than his own. This open attitude toward spirituality, free of exclusivity or judgment, was yet another thing the two men had in common.

Fumiaki was open to new ideas, too. This is what fueled his readiness to embrace and explore Buddhist thought and practice later in his life. While he had great respect for tradition, he was not overly attached to preconceived delineations or molds of spiritual practice. It was this personality trait that allowed Fumiaki and the master sculptor to bond, and that ultimately allowed Fumiaki to develop a new system of Buddhist practice.

By early afternoon the sky was completely clear, without a single snowflake falling. The taxi driver who had been waiting outside seemed glad about the weather after the difficult journey that morning. As Master and Mrs. Nakamaru said their goodbyes, Fumiaki carefully held up the statue of Achala. The Nakamarus' two young daughters, who were in the first and third grades, sat beside their mother in the car, as they were going to accompany Fumiaki back to Tachikawa. In their laps were statues of the Achala's two attendant bodhisattvas, Kimkara and Chetaka, that had been sculpted by their father.

After thirty or forty minutes during the drive back home, a five-colored iridescence, perhaps a cloud, hovered in the sky ahead of the car. It was an auspicious sign.

"Master, what is that?" Nakamaru's daughter asked Fumiaki. "Is it a five-colored cloud?"

"I don't know if it's a cloud or a rainbow," Fumiaki answered, "but it is mysterious."

The taxi reached Fumiaki's house in Tachikawa just after three o'clock that afternoon. Tomoji had been waiting anxiously and was glad to see them all arrive safely. "I was worried about the heavy snowfall," she told them, "but was relieved when it cleared so completely. Just an hour ago the sun even started to come out. It's unusual to have such a wonderfully quick change in the weather."

"It seems as if the clouds of delusion have all dispersed," Fumiaki replied. "There is not a single cloud in the sky."

Fumiaki and Tomoji placed the Achala statue in their alcove, enshrining it as appropriately as they could, given their modest surroundings. In his diary Fumiaki wrote, "To enshrine the Achala properly, I need a teacher to show me." All they could do at this moment, however, was celebrate with a dish of rice steamed with red beans, which is traditionally consumed during celebratory occasions.

After putting their children to bed, Tomoji turned to Fumiaki and asked, "For you to enshrine a buddha figure, don't you need to have a Buddhist name?"

"Yes, of course," Fumiaki answered offhandedly.

In Japan, Buddhist priests usually take a Dharma name different from their birth name. Fumiaki tried to act as if he had already thought of a proper priestly name, but Tomoji's question had been so sudden. Perhaps, having been distracted by the eventful day overall and particularly by Master Nakamaru's daughter pointing out the five-colored iridescence in the perfectly clear sky that afternoon, he didn't know quite how to respond at first. Finally, he said to her, "Well, you may know the phrase 'The clouds of delusion have dispersed and the sky has cleared.' What if I took the name *Tensei* (Clear Sky)?" Tomoji smiled with approval.

From that point on, Fumiaki began to go by the Buddhist name of Tensei.

II.

TENSEI

4.

Heeding the Call to Service

The First Winter Training

Since ancient times in Japan, aspirants have used the coldest time
of the year, from early January to early February, to conduct ascetic
training to purify negative forces and obstacles and spur the development of mental discipline and other spiritual faculties. Negative
forces needn't refer only to evil spirits. From a Buddhist perspective,
they can be thought of as outward manifestations of greedy, angry, or
ignorant thoughts and behaviors that produce suffering. These types
of negative energies prevent us from turning our hearts and minds
toward loving-kindness, and they act as obstacles on our path to spiritual liberation and enlightenment.

On January 8, 1936, Tensei and Tomoji were to begin a month-
long period of intense ascetic practice. Early each morning before
he left for the office, and each evening after he returned, Tensei and
Tomoji planned to dedicate themselves to practice. About thirty of
Tensei's Byozeisho devotees would participate as well.

But on the sixth of January, two days before they were to begin
their austerities, a member of Tensei's fledgling sangha invited a
monk from another Buddhist group to perform their first homa rite

in front of Achala. This member had it in mind to turn the Achala statue into a local attraction and hoped to build a large hall that would make the sangha famous in Tachikawa. Of course, his role would grow in prestige and power along with the fame of the Achala statue. The monk who had been invited to perform the rite boasted about himself instead of discussing the service, the Achala, or the people in the community. Tensei felt that these two men were only self-interested and looked at the Achala as an opportunity to gain some sort of power for themselves. "I noticed that the air around the altar seemed far from pure. It felt turbid—as though Achala himself were sullied," he later recalled.

Fortunately, others within the sangha offered Tensei their support. Grateful and buoyed by their fellowship, he reached out to his mentor, Shuko Obori, to see if he would request his Shingon esoteric Buddhist master, Hokai Urano, to come to Tachikawa to dedicate their "winter training" with another homa service at its conclusion. The master happily assented to do so. So it seemed that the bad omen of the circumstances surrounding the initial homa rite was allayed by the promise of a purer rite to follow. With this arrangement made, Tensei continued the month-long winter training.

The winter of 1935–36 was bitterly cold. At the time, most Japanese homes were heated with simple, not particularly efficient, coal braziers. A headline in a local newspaper that January read "Coldest Temperature Ever Recorded in the Capital." The article reported that "the air is bitter and the clear sky looks like a slab of ice. Water pipes and even local wells are frozen solid." In the middle of this frigid weather, every morning Tensei and Tomoji doused themselves with countless buckets of ice water and tirelessly performed special

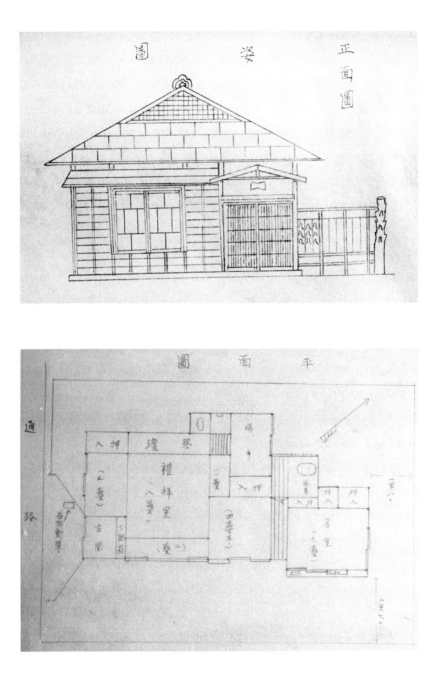

A sketch and the floor plan of the Ito residence at Nanko-cho, Tachikawa

prayer rituals to generate positive karma in the hopes of alleviating or transforming any obstacles to their congregation's spiritual practice.

Although they had not yet firmly established their practice system, during this very first training period they used the *Thousand-Scroll Sutra* practice, wherein participants chant the *Heart Sutra* one thousand times divided by the number of participants. The fewer the people, the greater the number of times they chanted. If only ten people gathered, for example, the group would recite the *Heart Sutra* one hundred times.

Tensei followed an extremely arduous regimen during the weeks of training. Day after day he engaged in difficult austerities. Years later one of Tensei's congregants, Mr. Sanjo Matsumoto, remembered bumping into Tensei during those early days and being startled by his appearance. "His face was extremely pale and each rib stood out like a knotted rope," he recalled. "He was but skin and bones, which made his arms and legs seem thin and elongated. He looked exactly like Shakyamuni during his days as an ascetic, or at least like the Buddhist texts describe his appearance."

Every day during the winter training, Tensei and Tomoji and a group of followers would begin to chant before dawn. On January 28, the day of the month when homa rites are usually held in Shingon temples, Tensei took the day off from work. In addition to the regular recitations at 5 a.m., the group performed a special round of chanting three hours later. They attracted an unexpectedly large group of people that day. Tensei wrote in his diary that he now felt he must follow a religious path so he could offer himself for their benefit and for the benefit of people like them. The Byozeisho was not enough.

The Decision to Leave Work

Tensei began thinking more and more about dedicating himself fully to his growing number of congregants. In his heart he was already inclined to live his life as a Buddhist priest, but actually embarking on a religious career is not that simple. One must affiliate with a temple and undergo religious training according to its tradition. That was but one of the decisions he would have to make.

Over the course of the month-long training, the number of requests that Tensei received for special prayers and consultations based on the Byozeisho increased so much that he was unable to accommodate every request, even if he completely filled up his weekends and weekday evenings. That first winter training made such an impression in the community that on the day of the dedicatory homa rite, just as the month-long practice was about to end, Tensei began to seriously consider leaving his job to serve the community full time. That day he wrote in his diary: "If I were to quit my job and become like a confidant to those in poverty (poverty in the spiritual sense, too), I would be more grateful and happier than I have ever been." Elsewhere he writes, "I reflected deeply on the question of whether I should leave my employer. I couldn't make a hasty decision about such an important matter, and many thoughts entered my mind."

Tensei's first concern was professional. He was part of a team of highly skilled, motivated workers charged with designing essential aeronautical equipment. Would his company even allow him to leave? But he also worried about the impact such a decision would have on his family. In *The Light in Each Moment* Tensei elaborates on how he felt, such as the importance of putting himself in the shoes of his wife, who was concerned about what would happen to his family if he no longer received a regular monthly income. He seriously questioned whether to give up his job for the benefit of other people.

A further complication for Tensei was that Ishikawajima Aircraft came under the control of the air force at a time when Japan was growing increasingly militarized. Airplanes were the military's star product, and as an aeronautical engineer, Tensei was highly valued and well paid. When Tensei's boss found out that he was thinking of quitting, he dismissed the idea, telling others, "We need him at the company! I'll be as fiercely determined as Achala! He absolutely cannot quit!"

With all of these issues weighing on his mind, on January 30 Tensei decided to discuss the matter with Tomoji. When he returned home that day she was busy preparing dinner. Chibun was on her back and their daughter was sitting by the hearth.

"So many people are seeking Byozeisho consultations these days. I just don't think I can keep up with both a secular and religious life," Tensei said. "I'm thinking of leaving my job at the aircraft company."

"That might be fine if you were alone," Tomoji replied, "but what about the children and me? You can't just quit."

Tensei was surprised at Tomoji's reaction, especially given her strong religious upbringing and spirituality. But as a young mother of two who expected an even larger family, her attitude was only natural. Tensei agreed to reconsider and tried to convince himself that he must find a different path. The following day the temperature dropped to the coldest measured in the area for nearly a decade. He went to work having decided that, for the time being at least, he was not going to resign.

While he was away at work, Tomoji too was having a change of heart. Tomoji had been raised by her grandmother, a practitioner of the *Lotus Sutra* and a spiritual adviser to others. Tomoji's aunt, Tamae Yui, had inherited her spiritual ability and had become a spiritual adviser herself. Perhaps Tomoji had also inherited some spiritual faculty from her grandmother. Whatever the case may be, after Tensei set out for work that day, Tomoji had a vision of Tensei dressed in a black monk's robe, sitting at the small table from which sutras are chanted, offering advice to people.

When Tensei returned home that evening, Tomoji told him, "You needn't worry about the children and me. If you won't be able to feed us all, I will take the children back to my hometown. Please, follow your religious path, even if it means you have to carry the Achala image on your back through the streets to collect alms. Achala will surely help you if you have such resolve."

But Tensei still could not decide. He began to worry more and more about the ramifications of leaving his job without any other source of income. That night he came to a point where he was set on keeping his job. He commented to Tomoji that it would be more painful to leave the company where he'd worked for the past seven years than it would be to part from his beloved children. The next day, on the first of February, Tensei received a call at work from Tomoji that their daughter had fallen ill with a high fever. He promptly returned home, where his wife confronted him: "You said that it would be more painful to give up your job than it is to part from your child. Now tell me honestly, which would really be more painful?" Tensei was at a loss for words. In that moment of clarity his mind was made up: he would leave his job.

Their daughter recovered from her fever within a few hours. The execution of his decision was postponed, however, as his boss persuaded him to take a leave of absence to reconsider his decision before making it final. He was persuaded to wait at least until the fiscal year was over, when he could collect his full severance pay. In the meantime, Tensei behaved as if the decision had already been made.

The Birth of a Spiritual Community

On February 3, 1936, Shuko Obori's Buddhist master, Hokai Urano, came to Tachikawa and led a dedicatory homa ritual to conclude the month-long winter training that Tensei and Tomoji had undertaken as their first formal religious endeavor after enshrining the Achala in their home. Hokai Urano was a devout practitioner of Shugendo in the Daigo school of Shingon esoteric Buddhism. Tensei describes him in his memoir as a strongly built man of about sixty, who was polite to everyone and very likeable. Master Yushu Okada, who later became head of the Daigoji Monastery, described Hokai Urano as an important priest with a sincere passion toward his practice.

Tensei had bought a rudimentary homa hearth from a Buddhist implements shop in Asakusa, east of Tokyo, and affixed it to the top of a temporary altar that a friend from the military days had made for him. The ritual commenced on schedule at 1 p.m., after lunch. Unlike the monk who had performed the initial homa rite, Reverend Urano conducted the rite according to established traditional procedures. To Tensei, Reverend Urano appeared to be in a state of profound mental concentration known as samadhi. Tensei would later record this homa ritual as the first to be performed before the Achala image after it was enshrined in his home, discounting the first rite altogether.

In the Shingon tradition, the acts of ascending to and descending from the officiant's seat to perform the rites are highly ritual-

The nascent spiritual community after their first homa ritual in front of the Achala image; Rev. Urano is in the center with Tensei sitting next to him on his left and Tomoji standing behind Tensei holding Chibun in her arms.

ized and are undertaken with deep reverence and humility. Tensei had no proper officiant's seat at his home altar, so Reverend Urano "descended" by removing the cushion he was sitting on. He then performed the final three bows and turned to face the congregation. He told them simply, "The homa is now complete." Even though the ceremony was performed with makeshift Buddhist implements, it greatly moved Tensei and all who were present.

As is customary on such occasions, Tomoji served chilled rice wine during the postceremony celebration. At that time the Reverend spoke to Tomoji at length, discussing her spiritual abilities and addressing some of her questions and uncertainties.

Five days later, on February 8, Tensei submitted his final letter of resignation. "It was as though the homa fire had burned away all doubts," Tensei later wrote. A fresh powdering of snow fell again in Tachikawa, an auspicious omen for Tensei and Tomoji as they stepped squarely onto a path of devotion to the spiritual care and well-being of others. At twenty-nine years of age, Tensei had now committed himself full time to his calling. Shinnyo-en marks February 8, 1936, as the day its path was born.

5.

Cultivating a Philosophy and Practice

Choosing a Tradition: Esoteric Buddhism

Having decided to spend the rest of his life as a confidant to those in need, Tensei resolved to find an appropriate Buddhist master under whose guidance he could properly train. His grandmother, Sono, who often recited sutras to him as a child, had drilled into him the importance of having a worthy teacher. Whenever they saw a monk asking for alms, she would teach Tensei how to recognize whether the person had been properly trained. But what was clearly foremost in all the religious knowledge Sono imparted to Tensei was the belief that it was crucial to find the right teacher. "Self-taught practice won't bring you the ability to guide and help others," she told him. "It's a dead end."

Decades later Tensei could see how true this was. Of course, every time he conducted a ritual he would do so with the utmost sincerity, but he knew he was not yet qualified to properly conduct such rituals alone. Whether he chose Shingon, Tendai, or some other Buddhist tradition, Tensei knew that it would be essential to receive Dharma transmission from a true master in that lineage.

Tensei greatly respected Hokai Urano, who by that time had become a trusted confidant. Reverend Urano had advised on how to organize the devotees that had gathered around Tensei and had also guided him on his Buddhist religious path. Tensei thought that he would become Reverend Urano's disciple, but the Reverend declined, saying that he wasn't qualified enough to take on that role. He knew that Tensei was intent on finding a good teacher of esoteric Buddhism.

In a diary entry from the day he resigned his position at the Ishikawajima Aircraft Manufacturing Company to pursue his religious career full time, Tensei had written that he believed esoteric Buddhism to be "the Buddhism of all Buddhisms," and "whether one can grasp its essence depends on having a good master." It was clear that Tensei wasn't interested in finding just a Buddhist master, but in finding one that could instruct him in Shingon esoteric Buddhism. Why did Tensei consider esoteric Buddhism to be the most highly developed Buddhism of all Buddhisms? To understand, we must familiarize ourselves with the tradition.

"The Buddhism of All Buddhisms"

After the historical Buddha, Shakyamuni, passed into final nirvana (parinirvana), the great religious community that he had worked throughout his life to establish began to crystallize into distinct subgroups because of linguistic and geographic differences that had developed within the group over the decades that the master had traveled and taught.

Over the course of centuries, there emerged two major factions within the Buddhist community—the more doctrinally conservative Theravada Buddhists, who based their practice on a set of scriptures preserved principally in the Pali language, and the more doctrinally liberal Mahasamghika Buddhists, who based their practice on a set of scriptures preserved principally in Sanskrit. There were many further subdivisions within these two groups as well. But these early Buddhist movements shared a very common set of doctrinal principles, or Dharmas, that allowed them to remain in common conversation with one another. These groups are sometimes referred to collectively as Abhidharma Buddhism because they shared a common philosophical dialogue with one another "regarding Dharma" (*abhidharma*).

Painting of Buddha Shakyamuni and his disciples
at the time of his transition into final nirvana

Around the beginning of the Common Era there emerged a Buddhist movement that embraced the idea of the path of the bodhisattva, or "buddha in training." Earlier forms of Buddhism accepted the idea that the Buddha himself had trained to become the Awakened One (Buddha) over the course of countless prior lives. The difference in this new movement, which called itself Mahayana Buddhism, was that its followers embraced the idea that they, too, could train to become buddhas at some distant point far in the future. They, too, could train as the Buddha was said to have trained in the tales about his previous incarnations. A series of new sutras that spelled out this idea began to appear and circulate among these early Mahayana Buddhists.

There is still much we do not know about the origins of Mahayana Buddhism. While Theravada and Mahasamghika devotees based themselves squarely in the tradition of celibate monasticism, Mahayana Buddhism seems to have involved not only celibate monks but also lay believers. Whereas the earlier Buddhist traditions emphasized personal religious training and enlightenment, Mahayana Buddhism made the pursuit of enlightenment one that benefited not only oneself but also others—a practice Shakyamuni himself had embodied as a bodhisattva. The term *Mahayana*, literally "Great Vehicle," refers to this altruistic motive for pursuing spiritual practice.

Adherents of the new Mahayana tradition began referring to pre-Mahayana traditions somewhat derogatorily as *Hinayana*, or "Lesser Vehicle," Buddhism—the idea being that a great vehicle made room for bringing others along to enlightenment as one travels the path of practice, whereas a lesser vehicle had room only for oneself. Many scholars believe that Mahayana Buddhism had its roots within the more liberal doctrinal positions of the Mahasamghika school and eventually grew to displace it altogether. Theravada Buddhism has survived since ancient times in the forms of Buddhism predominant today in Sri Lanka, Thailand, and Myanmar, and has more recently taken root in the West as well.

As Mahayana Buddhism grew in influence and spread throughout India, new sutras and treatises appeared that laid out the details of the spiritual path of practice and its philosophical underpinnings. One of the major ideas that Mahayana Buddhists emphasized was that buddhas are present in ways other than merely their physical form, and that these various manifestations of buddhas can bless and support fledgling bodhisattvas as they progress along the path. New buddhas associated with specific aspects of spiritual practice appeared in Mahayana texts and soon became objects of veneration for the tradition.

New Mahayana sutras appeared that systematically laid out the details of the lengthy bodhisattva path, largely structured around what are called the six perfections—generosity, ethical discipline, patience, heroic perseverance, concentration, and wisdom. As the community of Buddhists dedicated to practicing Mahayana grew, great trailblazers emerged who wrote seminal treatises on the system of practice and its philosophy, further establishing it as a legitimate path of Buddhist practice.

The Buddhist philosopher Nagarjuna was one of the trailblazers of Mahayana Buddhism in the second and third centuries. Nagarjuna compiled many of the Mahayana sutras and is particularly associated with the Perfection of Wisdom (*Prajnaparamita*) sutras and the notion of "emptiness" (Jpn. *ku*; Skt. *shunyata*). Nagarjuna taught that all beings and phenomena do not arise by themselves but always in relationship with causes and conditions, and so are insubstantial and empty of self-nature.

The philosophical tradition that grew out of Nagarjuna's thought is called Madhyamaka (Middle Way). Nagarjuna also helped to popularize the idea that many buddhas dwell in the past, present, and future and throughout the "ten directions" of space, and he systematized the bodhisattva's career of practice into ten stages.

Asanga, an erudite Buddhist monk who had trained in both the Hinayana and Mahayana systems of practice in the fourth century, was another major trailblazer of Mahayana Buddhism. Asanga is associated with the philosophical position that existence—the world, its inhabitants, we ourselves—is insubstantial, nothing more than a manifestation of consciousness. This philosophical view is referred to as *Chittamatra*, or Mind Only.

Asanga is also known as the author of the encyclopedic compendium of bodhisattva practice called the *Yogacharabhumi*, or *Stages of the Practice of Yoga*, which describes in minute detail every aspect of practice included in the Buddhist path, from taking refuge in the Three Jewels to the highest stages of meditative absorption. Given the fame and importance of Asanga's magnum opus, the tradition that grew up around his teachings is sometimes also referred to as the Yogachara school. Asanga's younger brother Vasubandhu, who was also an eminent scholar-monk, became a great master in this tradition, too.

Within Mahayana Buddhism, these two philosophical traditions, the Madhyamaka and Chittamatra, engaged in an ongoing philosophical debate. Mahayana thinkers constantly worked to resolve the dynamic tension between theory and practice, form and emptiness, the transcendent and the mundane, the enlightened and unenlightened, and universe and self. The movement that came to be known as esoteric Buddhism arose and began to flourish within this dynamic confluence of Mahayana Buddhist thought. In a sense, esoteric Buddhism represents a synthesis and resolution of the intellectual contradictions present in the two traditions of Madhyamaka and Chittamatra.

Out of the Mahayana idea that there are infinite buddhas and that they exist throughout time and space, esoteric Buddhists developed the notion of a primordial buddha or "buddha as an eternal principle of awakenedness within sentient beings." One such buddha is Mahavairochana (the "Great Sun or Illuminator"), the central figure of esoteric Buddhism. He is the apotheosis of Dharma or truth, an eternally unchanging, awakened presence that manifests within all beings in a way appropriate to each. In other words, Mahavairochana is both abstract and concrete, and because he is the manifestation of the universe in all things, he is also the self.[16]

It may seem that since Mahavairochana is the central figure of veneration for the tradition, an image of him would be enshrined in all temples related to esoteric Buddhism. But since every Buddhist divine figure is but an expression of Mahavairochana in a different form, it does not matter which buddha, bodhisattva, or luminous king (*vidyaraja*) is placed at the altar in a temple. This is why there are no fixed images that must be enshrined in the main halls of esoteric Buddhist temples.

Two core esoteric Buddhist texts emerged in the seventh century, the *Mahavairochana Sutra* and the *Vajrasekhara Sutra*. In the *Mahavairochana Sutra*, Mahavairochana approaches the important Mahayana concept of "emptiness" from an esoteric Buddhist perspective and thoroughly explains the nature of cosmic truth. In the

---

16. The personal pronoun "he" is used in this work, but in essence, Mahavairochana, like other transcendental Buddhist figures, is neither masculine nor feminine.

An image of Mahavairochana crafted by Shinjo in 1965

Vajrasekhara Sutra, Mahavairochana lays out how to grasp that cosmic truth through practice.

Moreover, both texts incorporated preexisting Brahmanic rites, like the homa, or "burnt offering," and other seemingly mystical practices, such as the recitation of mantras and the practice of yoga. The inclusion of such ritual practices has at its core a profound understanding that theory and practice are one. Theory exists only within practice, and practice exists only together with theory. In esoteric Buddhism all fundamental oppositions are dissolved, and success in practice is the attainment of this oneness.

We can think of esoteric Buddhism as a system of training that focuses on the acquisition of inherent, unrevealed wisdom that is inexpressible and can only be understood through direct, personal experience. This wisdom is considered esoteric because, although all sentient creatures are already intrinsically awake and possess buddha nature, they are ordinarily unable to access that spiritual knowledge within themselves or recognize their own nature.

The tradition is also considered esoteric because training involves taking part in rituals and practices that are only available to disciples upon initiation by a qualified teacher who has determined that they are ready to undertake the practice. Many aspects of the practice of esoteric Buddhism thus remain unrevealed to the uninitiated.

In the early ninth century, the Japanese master Kukai traveled to China, where the Chinese master Huiguo gave him the consecration rite, initiating him into the mandalas of the *Mahavairochana* and *Vajrasekhara* sutras. In the esoteric Buddhist tradition, everything in the world of Mahavairochana, the main transcendental buddha in esoteric Buddhism, is expressed within these two mandalas. Having

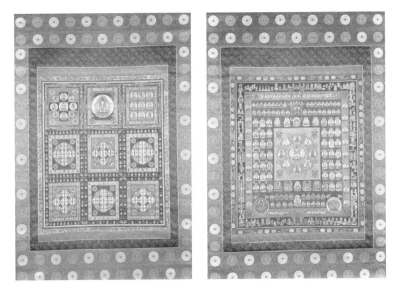

The mandalas of the *Vajrasekhara* (*left*) and the *Mahavairochana* (*right*) sutras that were offered to Shinjo by the Daigoji Monastery as an indication of his mastery of esoteric Buddhism. They are also known as the Diamond Realm Mandala and Matrix Realm Mandala, respectively.

trained under Huiguo, Kukai returned to Japan, where he established the Japanese Shingon school of esoteric Buddhism. Because Huiguo's principal Chinese disciple died unexpectedly, Kukai became the only person to fully inherit Huiguo's lineage of esoteric Buddhism. So the esoteric Buddhist lineage that passed from India to China and then to Japan ultimately remains alive only in Japan.

Since esoteric Buddhism was the last iteration of Buddhism to develop in India, and since it developed as the culmination of centuries of refinement of Buddhist thought, it is considered to represent the final, ultimate phase of Buddhist development. It is also considered superior to the other major systems of Buddhist practice in the sense that it synthesizes and resolves tensions and contradictions that appear in earlier Buddhist systems.

Esoteric Buddhism further set itself apart from earlier Buddhist traditions by the incorporation of esoteric ritual practices that are said to speed progress along the path to enlightenment. Whereas the Theravada tradition came to be called Hinayana, or the Lesser Vehicle, because of its focus on personal enlightenment, and the bodhisattva tradition came to be called Mahayana, or the Great Vehicle, because of its focus on enlightenment for the benefit of all beings, esoteric Buddhism came to be called Vajrayana, or the Diamond Vehicle, because its methods were unparalleled.

It is impossible to explain in simple terms the vast thought and system of esoteric Buddhism, but this extremely brief, simplified sketch of the formation and transformation of Buddhism that evolved over many centuries should give at least some idea of its history and context.

Each Buddhist tradition represented a serious attempt to engage with core philosophical issues. My intention here is not to debate their relative merits or to explain them fully. With this brief sketch, I hope readers can understand what Tensei likely meant when he wrote in his diary that esoteric Buddhism is "the Buddhism of all Buddhisms." Its teachings comprise a vast system that covers everything from the nature of the entire universe to the phenomena that appear before our eyes, and its theories synthesize all Buddhist thought and give them form and application in the practice of homa and other rituals, from which they are ultimately inseparable. Esoteric Buddhism represents the culmination of a millennium of Buddhist development in India and the pinnacle of Buddhist theory and practice.

Unity of Theory and Practice

Buddhist temples in Japan can be broadly divided into two types: those that principally exist to fulfill funerary functions for deceased family members of their congregants and those that principally exist to serve the everyday spiritual needs of living devotees via teaching and ritual. Most temples in Japan today are of the first type: locally established temples that exist to fulfill the funerary needs of the surrounding community.

The second type of temple, which focuses on the living, is sometimes called a devotee temple. Monks and priests at such temples attend to their congregants' needs by performing rituals and prayers to heal, support, and extend spiritual protection. Priests typically recite prayers and make requests on behalf of their congregants in front of a buddha image, such as a statue of Achala. There are, of course, temples that combine the two types of service. This kind of dual-purpose temple was what interested Tensei most. He wanted to provide traditional ceremonies like the memorial services and other rites, but it was also important that he lead his congregants to find personal peace as well. He felt called to respond to requests for prayer and to guide his congregants in their spiritual and practical needs.

Tensei in front of the sign "Fellowship of Light, an Affiliate of Naritasan"

Tensei's study of Shingon esoteric Buddhism led him to understand that ritual—even a ritual seemingly limited in the scope of its aims—is meant to benefit people in all aspects of their lives, not just in relation to one particular problem or illness. He felt that we shouldn't think of ritual only as a means of producing some immediate miraculous change in our lives—that may or may not happen. Instead we must understand the power that ritual has to provide direction, ameliorate disharmony within ourselves and between ourselves and others, and manifest a way of life that facilitates the development of our buddha nature.

Tensei taught that we cannot reduce ritual to mere technical competence or formalistic performance; rather, we must imbue ritual with the right attitude and effort for it to be effective. As Tensei matured as a spiritual teacher, he would frequently remind himself and his students that a spiritual pursuit for the sake of one's own interests is simply an assertion of the ego; we only really cultivate a true spiritual practice when we have dedicated ourselves wholeheartedly to the benefit of others. Ritual practiced with this type of altruistic attitude becomes one of the most potent and effective spiritual practices one could hope for.

Ultimately Tensei would use his teachings to reframe Buddhist practice as something people do for and with others, rather than as individual-focused personal training. For him, practice should not only cultivate one's own buddha nature, but should also help others to cultivate theirs.

Tensei's interest in promoting a ritual practice rooted firmly in a well-cultivated enlightened attitude placed him squarely within the long history of the Buddhist ritual tradition. Shakyamuni Buddha was said to be cautious of such ancient rituals because he believed they were focused on answering personal requests instead of helping a person move beyond the ego-self. He distrusted ritual as an end unto itself and always worked to ground ritual in deeper aspects of spiritual practice whenever he taught it.

Nowhere is the synthesis of ritual with spiritual practice more pronounced than in esoteric Buddhism, where theory and practice have been fused into one inseparable unit: theory exists only where there is a practice to demonstrate it and true practice exists only where it manifests theory.

Within ritual, where dharma manifests through our actions, we can relieve ourselves of negative emotions and desires, get outside of our "selves," and gain a clearer understanding that "self" does not exist in isolation—it is part of everything. By fusing theory and practice, doctrine and ritual, esoteric Buddhism dissolves the notion that Dharma and everyday life are fundamentally separate. This was the type of comprehensive practice that Tensei wanted to teach.

Homa: The Ritual at the Heart of Practice

Esoteric Buddhism employs a vast array of prayer rites to achieve its aims. Several of these are a type of ritual called *homa*, which is a Sanskrit word that means "burnt offering." Homa rituals are performed using fire and were an important practice in India long before Buddhism even existed. In their original Brahmanic context the purpose of homa was to burn offerings or a sacrifice in a fire, which would consume and transform the offering and convey it to the celestial realm in the form of fire and smoke, in return for which the gods would grant a request. In the context of esoteric Buddhism, the homa fire symbolizes the consuming and transforming power of wisdom, which completely burns away delusion and ignorance.

Although homa rituals may be performed to heal illnesses, to bring prosperity to a household, or to fulfill other mundane wishes, we shouldn't confuse them with prayer rites and prayers that are only intended to fulfill immediate desires. In some Japanese folk traditions, when one prays to heal an illness, one's objective in most cases is only to make the person well.

In esoteric Buddhism, however, even if we perform a rite to heal a person's illness, the objective of the ritual is never to simply heal the illness itself. From the perspective of esoteric Buddhism illness befalls us as a result of negative karma accumulated due to afflictions and

Tensei performing a homa ritual (c. 1937)

ignorance. Consequently, the homa rite is conducted to relieve the person of the conditions that cause illness or any type of suffering at all by burning away all of the person's afflictions. We seek to remove illness and other mundane problems because they become obstacles on the path to buddhahood and prevent awakening. No matter what the immediate aim of a homa rite may be, its ultimate goal is always the eradication of obstacles to enlightenment.

The Shingon homa rites that Kukai transmitted to Japan are categorized according to five different functions:

1. Those that are meant to remove the root causes of various calamities, from personal illness to natural disasters. These are probably the most commonly performed homa rites in Japan today and use a round homa hearth.

2. Those that are meant to bring prosperity and increase merit for both the individual petitioner and the community at large, including the nation. These homa use a square homa hearth.

3. Those that are meant to subjugate evil, subdue one's enemies, and ward off misfortune. These homa use a triangular homa hearth.

4. Those that are meant to bring love and respect. These homa use a homa hearth shaped like a lotus blossom.

5. Those that are meant to summon good fortune. These homa use a fire altar with an unusual diamond shape, called a *kongo* (*vajra*) homa hearth.

Shingon esoteric Buddhism actively incorporates these homa rites into the very heart of its practice, with the understanding that the goal of these rituals is to bring forth spiritual liberation for all beings in the form of freedom from attachment and other afflictions, negative karma, and suffering in general.

In other words, the real objective of ritual in Shingon esoteric Buddhism is to realize the intent of the buddhas: the spiritual liberation and awakening of all sentient beings. The tradition accomplishes this by practicing these rituals in such a way that the formal act of the ritual itself is indivisibly unified with and permeated by the wisdom that understands emptiness and interdependence. To see the prayer rites that make up the heart of esoteric Buddhist practice merely as means to fulfill mundane wishes is to miss the most crucial aspect of this system of thought.

When Tensei abandoned a rewarding profession in 1936 and followed an inner voice that told him to dedicate himself to the religious life for the benefit of others with no guarantee of success, he already knew he did not want to study Buddhism as a scholarly discipline alone. He chose to become a Buddhist who would live his teachings. For him, philosophy, principles, and practice had to be one. He already knew that he could use his knowledge and skill with the Byozeisho to offer consultation and advice to people who were suffering day-to-day challenges.

Tensei's decision to become a monk was born from his wish to truly be able to help address people's troubles at a more fundamental level rather than to merely combat them one by one as they arose. To do that, he knew he needed to offer more than just solace. Tensei realized that with a true mastery of Shingon esoteric Buddhism—"the Buddhism of all Buddhisms," with its rite of homa and other prayer rites backed by a systematized body of doctrine—he would be able to really benefit those who came to him for help.

Although Tensei had yet to fully articulate his beliefs in those early months of 1936, he had already begun to formulate them in his mind. An incident from that period illustrates how his systematic thought about the nature of true practice was beginning to take shape. Soon after welcoming the image of Achala into their home, after Tensei and Tomoji had begun their month-long period of winter austerities in the freezing weather, one of Tensei's colleagues at Ishikawajima Aircraft Company named Seikichi Igarashi visited Tensei. He told him that his brother had introduced him to another popular religious group in western Tokyo that was said to reliably grant all manner of wishes and that also had Achala as its principal object of devotion.

Based on his experience studying and working with the Byozeisho and his deepening understanding of the profound truths of Shingon esoteric Buddhism, Tensei was already acutely aware of how misguided and potentially damaging it was to use religion as a means to satisfy personal desires. He attempted to share his misgivings with Mr. Igarashi.

"I'm interested in a practice that will allow people to cultivate their own buddha nature, one that will help people help themselves," Tensei explained. "There are many kinds of spiritual practice," he told Mr. Igarashi. "Some people practice for personal benefit, some venerate sacred images, some seek spiritual guidance, and some desire simply to have their fortune told. But such practice will not change your life for the better. From now on, take refuge in what this Achala represents and forge a bright future yourself."

Mr. Igarashi was taken aback by this unexpected advice, but continued to practice with Tensei.

6.

Laying Foundations

Facing Difficult Social, Political, and Financial Conditions

Even before Tensei resigned from his job at Ishikawajima Aircraft, a group of informal patrons had formed around him to support his teachings and to practice them with one another. Groups that share the financial and spiritual support of their common religious practice are called *ko* in Japanese. The word *ko* originally referred to a gathering of monks who lectured on Buddhist sutras, but over time it has come to mean any group that shares a religious purpose.

Financial contributions from members of this group helped Tensei to purchase the Achala statue. Although the 300-yen honorarium that he paid for the sculpture was a remarkably modest price for an image said to be created by Unkei, it was by no means an inexpensive purchase for a young person in his position, particularly since he was about to leave his job. After selling his best camera, Tensei covered the remainder through contributions from his students who were interested in the Byozeisho.

At that point the group was only an unofficial ko, which was problematic, given the Japanese political climate in 1936. Social conditions had been steadily deteriorating throughout the decade as the Japanese government imposed strict controls on freedom of speech, ideology, and political association.

The Japanese secret police, called the Special Higher Police,[17] had become extremely powerful and kept a close watch over the activities of any religious or political groups. By 1936 the authorities took notice of all types of gatherings, even those held in ordinary, private homes. At first, arrests targeted only members of communist groups, but police raids against liberal, intellectual, and religious groups soon became common.

The Japanese government formally declared Shinto the national religion and began to suppress any newly established religious groups, which they said violated the Public Security Preservation Law. During the first few months of 1936 the secret police made examples of the popular religious organization Omotokyo and the Hitonomichi Church.[18] Omotokyo was ordered to disband and the Hitonomichi Church was closed down, its leaders arrested and its church buildings and stone statues dynamited. Thus they began a full-scale suppression of religious groups, culminating with the enactment of the Religious Organizations Law in 1939, which pressured religious groups to cooperate in the war effort. Given this environment, it would have been difficult and dangerous for Tensei and Tomoji to hold regular

---

17. The Special Higher Police force was established to investigate and control emerging political groups and ideologies that were deemed threats to public order. The passage of the Peace Preservation Law of 1925 gave the agency draconian powers, and it set up branches throughout Japan and in overseas locations with large Japanese populations, such as Shanghai, London, and Berlin.

18. Today known as the Church of Perfect Liberty, or PL.

gatherings in their home unless their group was officially recognized as a ko.

In addition to the challenging political environment, the abandonment of a well-paying, skilled job and devotion to the pursuit of a religious life brought social challenges to Tensei as well. People generally treated such life-changing decisions with suspicion. Even members of other religious groups in Tachikawa were wary, and no doubt a little resentful, of Tensei and the group that was growing up around him and the Achala statue.

Some scorned the group for their "suspect prayer rituals" and questioned Tensei's qualification and ability as a leader. "What good can a young company employee and layman like him possibly do?" "This unqualified person isn't even a recognized guide or leader, but he has enshrined Achala in his home!" Even some members of the sangha's executive board schemed against him, and neighbors with whom he'd had long relationships turned their backs on him. Tensei explains:

When I worked for Ishikawajima Aircraft, I earned a high salary. It is perhaps for that reason the neighbors seemed to respect and trust me. However, once I set out on a religious path and lost my company affiliation, their attitude changed. We were shunned by the community and endured endless discrimination. I became an outsider who had quit his job, enshrined an Achala, and—if they were to be believed—begun to propagate a dubious religion. In those days, the secret police were on the lookout for anything suspicious, and on more than one occasion we were fined for holding meetings without obtaining permission to form an association.

I had never expected that my new life would require so many cumbersome legal procedures. In those days, simply expressing a desire to help others was not enough to satisfy the civil authorities, and I could not hold any meetings without first having official approval. I did not belong to any recognized religious group, so I lacked the formal qualifications to teach and the official authorization to publicize our existence as a religious group.

On a more practical level, Tensei was also struggling to make ends meet. Mrs. Kuniko Nakamura, who lived two doors down from Tensei and Tomoji in Tachikawa, remembers the dramatic change that occurred in the Itos' lifestyle:

> Tensei had established a reputation as a gifted engineer at Ishikawajima Aircraft. His salary must have been substantial. They lived well and owned expensive furniture, so I had the impression that the Itos were quite wealthy. Then quite suddenly their lives changed and Tensei rapidly lost weight. I still remember my mother's reaction. She told me, "They were so well-to-do before, but now live so frugally. Amazingly, Mrs. Ito never complains."
>
> In those days, we shared a common well with Tensei's family. It seemed strange to me that Tomoji went to fetch water so many times a day. It was only much later that I learned they had left behind their secular lives to embark on a religious path, and that the water Tomoji drew from the well was used for ablutions.

By the spring of 1936 Tensei faced several challenges: he needed to obtain proper certification as a Shingon priest, fulfill the legal requirements that would make his group official, and feed his family. Despite these difficulties, the eight-hundred-year-old Achala image enshrined in the Ito home, Tensei's unique teaching of theory and practice, and Tomoji's spiritual abilities attracted an increasing number of people to the burgeoning religious group.

Becoming Affiliated with Naritasan Shinshoji

On February 13, 1936, Tensei visited Reverend Hokai Urano at his home in Zoshigaya in the Toshima district of Tokyo to ask for his advice. At the gate to Reverend Urano's temple hung a signboard that read, "Tenmei Fellowship, an Affiliate of Naritasan."[19] Tensei was welcomed into the Achala Hall on the second floor. There the twenty-nine-year-old sat solemnly before his mentor, nearly twice his age, to seek advice on the current state of affairs in Japan and the future of Tensei's spiritual community.

It was ten in the evening when Tensei left the Reverend's temple. The winter sky above the quiet residential lane was clear and full of stars. Tensei reflected on his conversation with the Reverend as he walked to Mejiro railway station. Unexpectedly, Reverend Urano had followed after him and called out from behind, "I was worried you might lose your way so I came to walk you to the station." Tensei felt that the Reverend had something more to say to him. As they walked together to the railway station, Reverend Urano talked to Tensei almost like a father who was worried about his son's future.

When they reached the station, Reverend Urano said, "You needn't worry about the Achala image. If you're really concerned, I suggest you dissolve your board. The group you have formed was an ad hoc committee anyway, meant to serve only until Achala was enshrined. So start anew. Remember, it's a new start."

---

19. The Naritasan Shinshoji temple complex, which also enshrines Achala as a principal image, is one of the best-known in the Tokyo area. This Shingon Buddhist monastery was founded in the tenth century and is located in the city of Narita (near present-day Narita International Airport), 60 kilometers east of Tokyo.

Reverend Urano and Tensei (c. 1936)

Reverend Urano watched Tensei board the train. Moved by his sincerity and concern, Tensei brought his palms together in a gesture of veneration and resolved to make a new start. Reverend Urano's advice must have seemed like a ray of light piercing the dark clouds before him. Though they had only met for the first time recently, they were already forging a deep bond. As Tensei returned home he kept repeating the Reverend's words over and over in his mind, "It's a new start."

The political situation in Japan continued to worsen. A few weeks later, on February 26, 1936, a cadre of 1,400 young military officers attempted a coup d'état in pursuit of a "Showa Restoration" to reestablish the emperor's authority.[20] They took over the Metropolitan

20. Named after the sitting emperor and modeled on the Meiji Restoration that had taken place seventy years earlier. Officers hoped that by rising up against what they

Police Department in Tokyo, the prime minister's official residence, and the private homes of leading government officials. They also killed or wounded several members of the cabinet. Nothing like it had ever occurred in modern Japan. Rumors ran rampant and the capital was thrown into a state of panic. Although the coup was quashed with the arrest of the rebel officers, the incident provoked the authorities to further tighten military rule. The sound of combat boots resounded throughout the city and religious oppression worsened.

About a month after Tensei's visit to Reverend Urano, the Reverend stopped by Tensei's home on his way back from Mount Takao. Tensei explained that he was deliberating about which teachers to practice under and also considering how best to organize the group of people who had become like his ko. Reverend Urano expressed his concern about the increasing power of the promilitary regime, and more specifically about the possibility of revolt among Tensei's board, which was mostly comprised of people who worked for Ishikawajima Aircraft.

Tensei asked Reverend Urano about his own temple affiliation. The Reverend explained that as a priest he belonged to the Daigoji Monastery in Kyoto, but that he had also received authorization from Shojo Araki, the chief abbot at Naritasan, to found and lead a ko affiliated with it. Reverend Urano suggested that Tensei also form a ko based at Naritasan.

"I think that you will ultimately have to enter the priesthood at Daigoji," he told Tensei. "But the most sensible approach is to receive authorization as an affiliate of Naritasan until you become independent."

---

termed "evil advisers around the throne" they would reestablish the emperor's authority. The attempted coup d'état came to be known as the "2/26 Incident."

The Reverend's advice sounded like a practical solution to Tensei. For more than a thousand years Naritasan had been synonymous with Achala in the minds of Japanese people. It seemed a natural place for Tensei's group to call home.

Naritasan Shinshoji was founded in Narita in 940 to commemorate a dramatic event. During an ongoing military revolt in eastern Japan, Emperor Suzaku dispatched the monk Kanjo to Kyoto to bring to eastern Japan a statue of Achala that had been enshrined at Jingoji, a Shingon monastery in Kyoto, and which was said to have been sculpted by Kukai himself. Suzaku hoped that peace could be secured by performing a homa in front of the Achala. When the uprising was successfully quelled, the Achala statue was permanently enshrined at Naritasan and the temple was subsequently given the name "Hall for Pacifying the Eastern Country."

Down through the centuries Naritasan became known for its Achala image. In the seventeenth century the kabuki actor Danjuro Ichikawa helped popularize the practice of visiting Naritasan. For many years Danjuro and his wife could not have children. But after he prayed at Naritasan, his son Kyuzo was born. Out of gratitude, he created a series of plays featuring Achala that attracted large audiences. Later, when Kyuzo was about to succeed his father in their kabuki lineage, he went to Naritasan and prayed for twenty-one days that he would become a great actor. From that time onward, the Ichikawas passed down their faith in the Narita Achala from one generation to the next.

The famous philosopher and economist Sontoku Ninomiya was also known for his devotion to the Narita Achala. In the first half of the nineteenth century Ninomiya practiced a twenty-one-day fast at Naritasan. He went on to lead a national agricultural revival and his name became synonymous in Japan with diligence and thrift. The association of Naritasan with these famous people and with Achala in the public imagination has made it a popular destination for both pilgrimage and short holidays. By 1936, Naritasan had for centuries been a mecca of those who have faith in Achala.

Considering Japan's social climate at the time, Reverend Urano's advice to affiliate his congregation with a well-established institution like Naritasan, rather than remaining independent, made a lot of sense to Tensei. Following his advice, Tensei disbanded his group of supporters on March 10, 1936.

Eighteen days later, after demonstrating his legitimate ownership of the Mahavairochana Achala image, Tensei registered his community as the Fellowship of Light (Risshokaku), a Tachikawa affiliate of Naritasan. At eight o'clock that evening, which was coincidentally Tensei's thirtieth birthday, the Fellowship of Light conducted a grand homa in front of its Achala image.

Tensei (*center*) with members of the Fellowship of Light on their first visit to Naritasan Shinshoji

On May 16, Tensei led forty-three members of the newly established Fellowship of Light, along with Reverend Urano and members of his fellowship, on a trip to Naritasan. There he completed the paperwork to formalize the creation of the Fellowship of Light.

Two days later, again accompanied by Reverend Urano, Tensei set off for Kyoto on the night train to begin his formal training as a Buddhist monk. The following day he was ordained at Daigoji, taking the precepts under the direction of the ninety-sixth abbot of the temple, Egen Saeki. His priestly name was Tensei, but now he was also Tensei, a Shingon esoteric Buddhist monk. At the end of the following month, on June 29, the abbot and denomination leader at Naritasan, Shojo Araki, officially confirmed the Fellowship of Light as an affiliated temple.

Choosing to Train at Daigoji in Kyoto

When it came time for Tensei to choose where to undertake his training, the most obvious solution would have been to study at Naritasan, with which he had already formed the Fellowship of Light as an affiliate. But Reverend Urano advised against it. Although Reverend Urano had a ko affiliated with Naritasan, he was also a Shugendo practitioner in the Daigo school of Shingon. He thought that the better choice for Tensei to receive initiation into various prayer rites would be Daigoji in Kyoto. Daigoji also oversaw the Tozan tradition of Shugendo.

Since Tensei wanted to learn both the philosophy and practical training of esoteric Buddhism, including the intricacies of its rituals, Reverend Urano believed that Tensei would benefit from training and practicing at Daigoji. Tensei deeply wanted to help people cultivate buddhahood, but also recognized that people have everyday problems with which they must contend in order to be able to achieve spiritual growth. Knowing that he could help his students meet their everyday challenges only if the rituals he conducted on their behalf were backed by a well-established system of Buddhist teachings, he agreed that a Shingon monastery like Daigoji would be good for him to learn what he needed to be a successful teacher.

The five-story pagoda at the Daigoji Monastery

The Daigoji Monastery in Kyoto was founded in 876 by Shobo, also known as Rigen Daishi, who was a disciple of Kukai's younger brother, the Shingon patriarch Shinga. Daigoji is known for the emphasis it places on the doctrine and prayer rites of Shingon, and their inseparability. The monastery is divided into upper Daigoji, situated at the top of Mount Kasatori, and lower Daigoji, spread out across the base of the mountain. The grounds cover approximately 6.6 square kilometers, with most of the mountain dedicated to the temple's precincts, and is located southeast of Kyoto in the southern part of the Yamashina valley. It is home to Kyoto's oldest wooden structure, a five-story pagoda inaugurated in 951, as well as 150,000 precious objects. It is cherished today as a museum of esoteric Buddhist culture and has been a UNESCO World Heritage Site since 1994.

7

Transformed by Suffering and Hardship

The Young Couple Build a Practice amid Scarcity and Want

Within a hundred days of resigning from his job as an aircraft engineer, Tensei had gained official religious status as a monk affiliated with a Buddhist monastery that had a tradition going back more than a thousand years. He had formed an official ko and was appointed its leader. It was a dramatic change that reflected the power of his own will, and perhaps the will of the buddhas.

Nevertheless, despite all they had accomplished, these were uncertain times for Tensei and Tomoji. In addition to increased government scrutiny, they also faced difficulties on a practical level due to Tensei's sudden loss of income. As Tensei later recalled in a diary entry:

We plunged into an unknown world. It truly was uncharted territory. Up until that day I enjoyed a steady income that had kept us financially secure, but now we had no idea how we were going to pay the rent or take care of our daily expenses. We had never lived with such uncertainty. Convinced that everything would become clear as we walked the path with buddhas, we set out to unveil an unknown world, little by little. Day after day, from early morning until well after midnight we engaged in one religious practice after another. We hardly had a spare moment to worry about our livelihood. Of course nothing in this world is free, and soon we were down to our last grain of rice.

While Tensei was constantly engaged in the practice of austerities, there was barely enough food for the family to eat. Fish hardly ever appeared on their dinner table, and according to Tomoji, for two years the Ito family could not afford a single sardine. The only snacks their young children ever ate were leftover, broken pieces of candy that had served as offerings on the altar. Although Tensei's will to follow the path of the buddhas had not wavered, we can only imagine the pain the situation caused him as a parent.

When he took that first trip as the leader of his community to Naritasan, he had to borrow a robe from Reverend Hokai Urano. It was the first time Tensei had ever needed formal Buddhist garb. According to Tensei, he struggled to put it on at the shop that served as the inn where the group stayed, which was so crowded with departing and arriving pilgrims that it resembled an overflowing train car. He looked disheveled and his left sleeve was rolled up in an awkward way. So when he entered the precincts of Naritasan, the leaders of other groups, drunk on sake, mocked him, saying to one another, "Look at that funny-looking young monk!"

Two days later, when Tensei and Reverend Urano returned on the night train to Kyoto for his ordination, Tensei could not afford the 30-yen cost of suzukake robes. He couldn't even afford 6 yen for a ritual mashikon surplice. The Reverend was wearing the only robes he owned, so in the end the Daigoji administrative office lent Tensei a robe and surplice, just in time for him to participate in the ceremony.

Even amid such poverty and other difficulties, Tomoji's determination never wavered either. She, more than anyone else, ministered to the needs of the growing number of people who gathered in their small home, while also taking care of her own household. One long-time apprentice recalls coming to the house each day before breakfast to help her care for the baby. Tomoji would always say to him, "You must be hungry. Please eat." He knew that if he accepted the offer Tomoji would miss a meal herself, so he refused. But Tomoji would insist, telling him, "I know you are hungry, despite what you say."

Tensei had confidence in Tomoji not only as a good wife and mother, or even as a valued partner in caring for the members of the Fellowship of Light. He knew that she possessed unusual abilities and that she had inherited spiritual gifts from her grandmother and aunt, who had both been practitioners of the *Lotus Sutra*. Tomoji had been crucial to Tensei's decision to pursue a religious life. From the day they welcomed the Achala statue into their home, her spiritual abilities had grown more and more evident.

Tensei wrote in his diary that a strange thing happened to Tomoji the first day they enshrined the Achala at their place. Her two hands, pressed together in gassho, rose above her head to form another *mudra*. The thumbs and little fingers of her two hands touched to make the mudra. After a few moments, her hands returned to their original position. But she repeated the same movement several more times. Tomoji had no way of knowing that she had formed an esoteric Buddhist mudra called the "lotus mudra."

Tomoji had already entered a state of oneness with Achala, which only seemed to grow stronger in the days that followed. So throughout the course of his esoteric Buddhist training, as Tensei worked to bring the Byozeisho system of spiritual discernment into the esoteric Buddhist system of teachings, he also incorporated Tomoji's spiritual abilities into his practice. He believed Tomoji's spiritual faculty would be meaningful only when it was placed in a doctrinal framework.

Bearing the Unbearable: The Loss of a Child

Despite the political and legal uncertainty that surrounded them and the financial struggles they faced inside the home, Tensei and Tomoji's life was continually brightened by their love for their firstborn son. Chibun's toddling playfulness brought great comfort and joy to the young couple. As Tensei recalled:

> Since we had taken up our religious vocation full time, our program of continuous religious practice, day and night, from dawn until dusk, had pushed us to our physical limits. We also found ourselves suddenly poor. Our life was as desolate as a winter field. Amid these circumstances, the innocent behavior of Chibun, not yet two years old, was our source of joy. From a material point of view, our new life of spiritual pursuit was like walking in an arid wilderness. But Chibun's innocent smile and lovable gestures were the light of our lives.

In late May 1936 Chibun got sick. At first it seemed that he just had a cold, but his symptoms didn't improve. He wasn't the only one in their community who was ill at the time. "There are too many sick people," Tensei wrote in his June 5, 1936, diary entry. "Those who came to ask us for help were all sick, some with tuberculosis, others

Photo of Chibun on Japan's traditional Boy's Day, May 1935

with pneumonia, rheumatism, and children's dysentery. During the day, we attend to those who seek our help, and at night, instead of sleep, we take care of Chibun and perform prayer rites for him. Though we regret that we have too little time for it, we also continue to chant the *Heart Sutra* and mantras."

Nowadays when people fall ill, they visit a hospital, not a monk. But during those days even large cities had few hospitals. When people fell ill, it wasn't unusual for them to go to a religious practitioner to request the performance of prayer rites to restore their health.

While Chibun's cold-like symptoms came and went, others who visited Tensei to ask for prayers appeared to be getting well. Some began to say that Chibun was absorbing the misfortune of their illnesses into himself. Tomoji asked Tensei to perform the rite of the Five Luminous Kings for Chibun. Earlier that year Reverend Hokai Urano had transmitted the rite to him. So, Tensei performed the rite for several days.

On June 8, Chibun's pulse was steady and he appeared to be getting better. Tensei waited until midnight and then performed the final homa rite. After he finished, Tensei, perhaps sensing that Chibun's condition was not really improving, took his little body in his arms and held him.

After some time, choking back tears, Tensei handed him back to Tomoji. He came down from the homa platform, sat in front of Tomoji, and gazed at little Chibun, who was gasping in pain. He put his hands on his wife's shoulders, telling her quietly: "The one who is grieving with you, the one who is weeping with you, is Achala, the embodiment of awakening that you believe in. Quietly look at the face of Achala and let us cry out to him to liberate us from our sadness, from this painful state! Let us plead, let us pray! Mantras are 'true words' that are cries of the 'true heart.' Be calm, and with this mantra of Achala that gushes forth from the true heart, let us throw ourselves upon his loving-kindness until we can let go of all our distress."

Hearing this, Tomoji looked up at the Achala statue. Gripped by a feeling she could not put into words, she wept as she chanted the mantra. On June 9, 1936, Chibun's young life came to an end. Thirteen years after Chibun's death, Tomoji remembered that day:

I quietly turned to look up at the Achala and was struck by a feeling I couldn't express. All I could do was chant the mantra with tears in my eyes.

Suddenly I felt an ethereal shock in my hands that were holding Chibun—the end was near. I felt it, and without thinking, I stopped chanting the mantra and started to cry, "My baby! My baby!" Maybe he became aware of my voice on his cheek, because he let out a painful cry. As I cradled him in my lap he entered a deep sleep, setting off to the other world.

Despite having heard all the teachings, as a young mother whose beloved child was made to bear such a heavy burden, I was confused. Surely he was not ready to die and wanted to stay for a long, long time on his mother's breast. I knew I had to embrace what I believed the buddhas were presenting to me, but as a young mother who had to let go of her dearest son—who was bearing such a burden—it was so hard.

Neither Tomoji nor Tensei ever forgot that day. Nor did they ever forget Chibun, even though his stay was brief. Tomoji was a young mother of only twenty-four. To suddenly lose her child in that way tore her heart. Tensei recalls Tomoji's state at that time:

> It had been four months since she gave up everything and began to walk this path, and the first thing that happened was to be struck with the grief of her beloved child's death. "Do the buddhas have no compassion? Can the buddhas be so cruel? What is the buddhas' compassion, anyway?" My wife asked these questions in agony, mired in grief.

These are the questions many of us ask when unbearable misfortune befalls us. What is the buddhas' compassion anyway? When the unthinkable, the unimaginable, death of a beloved child happens, we are shaken and wonder. This kind of profound tragedy can lead a person to be overwhelmed, to give up on life, or to become hopelessly cynical. Tensei took it as an opportunity to strengthen his resolve to serve others. Tomoji, a new mother with such profound love for her child, was torn between her faith in the buddhas and her overwhelming grief. Chibun's death was a blow that the young couple would carry in their hearts forever. But it also kindled within them an inextinguishable resolve to carry on with their mission of helping others come to terms with life as we know it.

As Tomoji wrote in *The Path of Oneness*:

On June 9, 1936, I prayed and prayed as I held Chibun, who had borne such a heavy spiritual load for us. Although I wanted so much to pray for his recovery, it was also my responsibility to guide those who continued to suffer from the influences of negative forces that arose from thinking only of themselves. I realized that to become able to guide them out of the bondage of such forces, I had to be the one to break the chain and develop my own spirituality.

In the past, Tensei had often told me about transforming adversity into a blessing, like a farmer pulling weeds and turning them into compost to enrich the soil. I shuddered as I watched Chibun purse his lips and moan in a way that reflected the terrible spiritual influences on him. Desperate to save my baby, I was tempted to beg for spiritual favors, only to pull myself back at the last moment.

The experience of parting with one they loved so dearly transformed Tensei and Tomoji into people who cared for others just as they would for their own children. In losing their young child they became "Dharma parents," caring deeply for those who came to them for guidance. Tomoji wrote:

Had I not completely believed in my husband's words, but instead allowed the weeds of my ego to bind me to thoughts only of my child, neither my soul nor my baby's would ever have found true peace. Tensei, too, would have been destined to either suffer in this life or to languish in a world of suffering after death. The death of Chibun was a severe blow, but the very enormity of the loss lit an undying flame in my soul. That flame has made me able to walk hand in hand with others in this world of suffering so that they may also touch the limitless loving-kindness and compassion of buddhas. I owe this all to Chibun, and for that I am truly grateful to him.

Deep in grief, Tensei and Tomoji used their son's life and his death to further inspire them. Chibun was given the posthumous Buddhist name *Kyodoin*, "One Who Guides to the Teachings." His sudden passing marked a new beginning for the sangha that Tensei had been building. Years later, Tensei wrote about the meaning of Chibun's death:

> Before Chibun died, we had to grope and search to find our way. But after his death, things began to fall into place one by one. Our grief enabled Tomoji and me, as people devoted to religious life, to overcome our human motives that put the happiness of those we love the most above our concern for all others. Most of our students at the time were seeking a path of practice to gain some personal reward, such as prosperity in business or recovery from illness. That is why, initially, I would perform healing rites and pray to satisfy their personal requests before attempting to guide them to seek the path for their spiritual growth. Even then, no one listened to my guidance; they just wanted their wishes fulfilled.
>
> As the child's posthumous Buddhist name suggests, people began to change after Chibun's death. They began to reflect on their self-serving motives in pursuing spiritual practice and adopted a more buddha-centered mindset. At the same time, as a spiritual guide, Tomoji was now able to immediately enter into a deep state of meditation and provide the type of verbal spiritual guidance that forms the basis of present-day *sesshin* meditative training.
>
> I believe that the collaborative efforts of Chibun in the spiritual realm and our efforts in this world produced wondrous results in our quest to

inspire practitioners to pursue the path toward awakening. Practitioners awoke more to the truth of things as they are, and the Shinnyo path began to take firm root in Tachikawa.

In his teachings, the Buddha frequently spoke of impermanence—the idea that change is constant, nothing remains the same, and nothing is eternal. While it is undeniable that at some point we will be forced to experience the heartbreak of parting with loved ones, we have the power to change the way we perceive such tragic events and can choose how we act in response to them.

Meditating on and becoming familiar with impermanence, however, does not diminish our sorrow when we lose a loved one or remove the pervasive sense of loss when they are gone. Yet Tensei and Tomoji's experience demonstrates that even in the darkest of times we can overcome and not be overwhelmed. We can even use painful experiences to foster spiritual growth—for the benefit of others rather than for self-serving purposes—as we develop the buddha qualities of loving-kindness, compassion, and wisdom that are innate in us all.

Tensei and Tomoji's example shows us how every event in our lives carries in it the potential to inspire deeper insights. This kind of positive shift in the perception of impermanence and change helps to motivate us to move forward with renewed purpose and drive. The inspiration that awakens us to this truth is a manifestation of what can sometimes seem to be the "merciless" love and compassion of buddhahood. The experience of being parted from one they so dearly loved transformed Tensei and Tomoji into people who cared for others just as they did for their own child.

Many years later, Tensei and Tomoji's daughter, Shinso Ito, spoke of how her parents reacted to the death of her brother:

> My father instructed that all items used by Chibun be kept out of his sight because he could not bear the memories they conjured up. I think the pain he felt would have been different had they been a little more affluent and able to do more for Chibun. But my parents lost everything—even spare time to spend with their children—after they embarked on the religious path. All that Chibun had was a Buddhist staff with which to play in the corner of the room. I think the sorrow that my parents felt for Chibun was that much greater because they felt they had been unable to do all they could for him.

Chibun's funeral was held on June 10, the day after he died, in the drizzling rain at Tensei and Tomoji's home in Tachikawa. It was attended by three priests from Fusaiji, an old Rinzai Zen temple nearby. Tensei and Tomoji could not afford to give him a proper burial, so through one of their students, who acted as an intermediary, they had his cremated ashes temporarily placed at a Pure Land temple in the Senju neighborhood of central Tokyo.

Tensei closed the doors of the encasement that housed the Achala statue for the funeral. Before reopening them, he and Tomoji began waterfall training at the Jataki waterfall on Mount Takao. After the evening service ended in their home, they would take the last train to Takao and begin the training at about two in the morning, then return on the first morning train to perform a homa service at the temple. "We undertook the waterfall training as a way of making a new start," Tensei later wrote.

Shinjo training at the Jataki waterfall on Mt. Takao (c. 1950)

The first time they conducted the demanding waterfall meditation training was on June 14, 1936, five days after Chibun's passing. Back then the water fell in far greater volume than it does today
and landed with such force that anyone who ventured under it was
almost instantly pushed aside. Moreover, the water was so cold, even
in summer, that a person's teeth would rattle until they couldn't
speak. Nevertheless, Tensei and Tomoji both prevailed. Tomoji
intoned the *Goreiju*[21] with a clear, penetrating voice that seemed to
shake the rocks around her. She would raise her arms high above her
head to repel the fierce water as she formed the lotus mudra.

The first few times, Tensei and Tomoji had difficulty walking up

21. In Shinnyo-en, *Goreiju* refers to the Mantra of Achala's Benevolence and Liberation, which is chanted to the melody that Chibun imparted to Tomoji at the time of
his passing.

the mountain to the falls, but later they found a shortcut, although they still had to negotiate 4 kilometers of rough terrain. It was early summer, the beginning of the rainy season, and the rain that had been falling steadily since the previous day had increased the force of the waterfall. But they safely completed their chanting under the cold water. Anyone who has ever sat below a waterfall can understand the sense of something happening beyond oneself.

Tensei's carving of Achala (1937)

At the start of the annual winter training, near the beginning of the following year, in 1937, Tensei began to sculpt a relief of a seated, cross-legged image of Achala. Although years later he would become known as the "Buddhist master sculptor of the Showa era" because of his prolific output of Buddhist images, this was the very first Buddhist image he created. Perhaps Tensei sought to help himself overcome the grief of Chibun's death by carving the "unwavering (achala) mind" that led to faith. Or perhaps he felt that by carving the Buddhist image as a prayer for Chibun, he could give the "unwavering mind" of faith in his own buddha a tangible form.

Forging Ahead in a Treacherous Climate

In 1937, the crackdown on unauthorized religious groups only worsened when Japan plunged into all-out war with China. In the name of emergency wartime conditions, ordinary speech and thought were subject to government control. Whenever more than ten people gathered in one place, they had to submit a report to the local police. Tensei's home was not a temple or a church, although his group was now officially associated with Naritasan. Yet among people outside the group, gossip circulated that the group's leader was a layman with no experience who had quit his job and become a "ritual master." "He's young, but the rituals he performs are powerful," people whispered.

There was some truth to the gossip, of course. Tensei had been given the nickname "Admirable One of Tachikawa," and people were constantly coming to his home to consult with him about their problems. Tensei offered them advice based on the Byozeisho, and for those who requested it he also performed prayer rites on their behalf.

Yet religious freedom was becoming more and more difficult in Imperial Japan. An incident occurred in February 1937 when a simple, unexpected gift to the Fellowship of Light created problems with the police. Masakichi Kubota, who ran a local inn in Tachikawa, donated a stone statue of Achala. In the world of Buddhist art, this type of statue—created not by a Buddhist master for a temple but by a devout, ordinary citizen as a personal object for prayer—is called a "folk buddha," or *minkan butsu*. After consulting Tomoji, Tensei decided to place the statue just outside the entryway to their house. That way those who might not be so interested in actually practicing could still pay their respects as they passed the house.

The stone image of Achala

Tensei should have known better, particularly after a visit to Reverend Urano, who warned Tensei that he should be careful because suddenly placing a buddha image outside his temple could give the authorities a reason to interrogate him. Sure enough, on March 5, about a month after Tensei had placed the stone image outside his house, a police officer visited him and ordered that the statue be removed. The officer said that Buddhist statues could not be placed in front of a building that was neither a temple nor a church. Strictly speaking, Tensei wasn't even allowed to have people gather in his home.

The policeman asked Tensei what kind of religious gathering was conducted in his home. Tensei thought everyone in the neighborhood already knew, so he replied that they belonged to the Shingon tradition. But the police officer wasn't satisfied, saying, "You say you are part of the Shingon tradition, but that's very vague. What exactly is your affiliation?" Tensei responded that he had received ordination in the Daigo school of Shingon Buddhism, was currently undergoing further training, and that last June his group had become an official affiliate of Naritasan under the name of Fellowship of Light, of which he was the head. Fortunately, the officer's mother was a devout practitioner of Naritasan, and that seemed to satisfy him. He told him that in that case, he only had to register the group with the city police headquarters as a religious association.

Four days later, on March 9, Tensei registered with the police as an affiliate of Naritasan and the affair was put behind them. Once again Tensei was glad to have had the advice of Reverend Urano, whose idea it had been for the Fellowship of Light to become affiliated with this well-known, respected temple complex.

After the policeman had ordered him to remove the Buddha statue from outside his house, Tensei began to think of the statue, which had been hewn from an old grindstone, as a metaphor for his current situation. Religious practice is not unlike a grindstone: one can use it to polish oneself. The hardship of losing his son and the uncertainty of the political climate were challenges that Tensei could use to polish away his own human impulses and build up his practice. The stone statue of Achala still stands at Shinnyo-en in the courtyard at Shinchoji, Shinnyo-en's foundational temple building in Tachikawa.

While Tensei's group was not subject to government control as a new religious movement, this was a time when every kind of gathering attracted the attention of the special political police, and Tensei recalled that the social climate intimidated people from attending his services and that he was not allowed to pursue religious activities as he wished. Many people, however, were undeterred and continued to come to Tensei's home to ask for prayer rites to be performed on their behalf. In addition to worries about the changing social and political climate, Tensei found that he also had to be wary of certain members of his own group's executive board. These were primarily the financial backers of the Fellowship of Light, who periodically tried to profit from the fledgling sangha.

Shortly after Chibun's death, one such board member, out of self-interest, pressured Tensei to make a temple in the neighboring city of Akishima a branch of the Fellowship of Light. At the time this temple was derelict and lacked any resident priest. Although Tensei was undoubtedly aware of the difficulties of having to restore and administer an abandoned temple, he reluctantly took the board member's advice. On the first anniversary of Chibun's passing, Tensei had his ashes transferred from a temple in Senju in eastern Tokyo to the one in Akishima.

Tensei almost immediately regretted the decision. The temple in Akishima was in a sad, dilapidated state. The longtime Shinnyo-en practitioner Kyuroku Shindo described the temple as "a humble place . . . No, impoverished is a more accurate description. His (Chibun's) plot was a flat, nondescript patch of land randomly fenced off with nothing but a single wooden pole at its center functioning as a temporary marker. With Chibun's remains laid to rest in such a desolate place, I could hardly bear to lay eyes on it."

In his journal, Tensei apologized to his son:

> I cried out to him in my heart, "Chibun, we may have to place you here for a while, but I promise we will move you somewhere else! Please be patient for just a little while. I'm sure you must feel sad and lonely for the moment, but please bear with us until we can properly lay you to rest."

But not everything was going against Tensei and Tomoji. On April 8, 1937, ten months after Chibun had passed away and on the date that is celebrated as the Buddha's birthday in Japan, Tensei and Tomoji experienced a happy event when their second son, Yuichi, was born.

Tomoji with Yuichi, the Ito family's second son

8

Growing a Community around Achala

Lore Associated with Achala Gazing Straight Ahead

While Tensei was undergoing training at Daigoji, talk of his Achala statue piqued the interest of some of the monks there. One of these was a master named Shojin Ono, who had initiated Tensei into a number of different rites, including the homa rite. Ono oversaw upper Daigoji, the part of the monastery up on the mountain. When Tensei related how the sculptor Odo Nakamaru had passed the image on to him, Ono expressed surprise that the statue had found its way into the hands of a private civilian outside of a monastery. Tensei's description of the details of the statue, such as its crystalline eyes and hollow neck area that contained something within, substantiated its attribution to the period in which Unkei was active. Pressed for more details by Ono, Tensei explained that while Achala's expression was as fierce as any Achala image, it also looked as though he was holding back tears. This seemed to convince Ono that the statue was likely to be Unkei's creation.

"Unkei carved very few Achala statues with both eyes open, looking straight ahead!" he told Tensei excitedly. "You don't see many Achala images with both eyes looking straight ahead anyway, whether they were created by Unkei or not."

Ono noted that the fierce yet tender facial expression of such Achala images showed the great compassion hidden behind the wrathful countenance. "When a father cries," he added, "he maintains a powerful gaze. He tries to weep only in the depths of his eyes, not at the surface. That's how Unkei sculpted Achala's expression. If your statue is indeed such a creation, then what's inside the hollow neck must be an actual relic of the Buddha."

Ono then surprised Tensei, telling him that according to legend those who come to own an Achala statue that gazes straight ahead are destined to found a new school of Buddhism.

"I would never presume to do such a thing," Tensei responded, "but it is indeed quite a wonderful Achala."

It is certainly true that statues of Achala gazing straight ahead are not common. The best-known examples of these include the

The Achala enshrined at Shinchoji temple

Wave-Cutting Achala, housed at Kongobuji Monastery on Mount Koya, which Kukai himself is said to have sculpted. Then there is the Achala at Negoroji, founded by Kakuban, and the Achala that Unkei sculpted, housed at Ganjojuin. Statues like these are mainly attributed to the early part of the Heian period, from 794 to 1185, the last division of classical Japanese history. Until roughly the ninth century, Achala was depicted with a forward-looking gaze, but that mostly stopped when the Buddhist priest Annen of Godaiin Monastery on Mount Hiei delineated nineteen characteristics of Achala images in a manual of rites and procedures he authored. Since then most Achala images depict him with a fierce expression, with the right eye gazing up to heaven and the left staring down at the earth.

The belief that a person who possesses a forward-gazing Achala statue will found a new school of Buddhism likely comes from the fact that both Kukai, the founder of Shingon esoteric Buddhism, and Kakuban, who started the New Shingon movement, both possessed this type of statue. According to Buddhist lore, Kukai carved an Achala from a piece of sacred wood that his master Huiguo had given him. Huiguo then consecrated the statue. As the story goes, when Kukai returned to Japan from China in 806, his ship encountered a storm and shipwreck seemed imminent. Kukai prayed for help, and Achala appeared wielding his flaming sword, which he used to cut through the waves and subdue the weather. Kukai's statue came to be called the Wave-Cutting Achala as this legend circulated orally.

The most famous anecdote about Kakuban's forward-gazing Achala is the story of the Pierced Achala. Kakuban sought to reform the Shingon Buddhist tradition, but the resident monks at Kakuban's monastery, Kongobuji, opposed his actions. A group of them burned down part of the monastery and tried to drive Kakuban out of

Kongobuji. They forced their way into the Achala hall, where Kakuban had secluded himself, but when they burst into the room he was nowhere to be seen.

Instead, they saw two Achalas, both engulfed in flames. Only one was the Achala enshrined in the hall. Kakuban's Achala was rare in that both eyes were open, his gaze fixed straight ahead. The other Achala that confronted the crowd was said to be Kakuban in meditation, in such a deep state of oneness with Achala that he had taken on the buddha's physical form. The monks tried to smash both Achala figures, but the intense flames forced them to keep their distance. They then threw stones at the two images, but not even one reached them. Finally, they used an awl to see what would happen if they stabbed either Achala in the knees. Surely the one who was really Kakuban would bleed. According to the legend, however, both images began to bleed when stabbed. Seeing this, the monks trembled with fear and fled.

Tensei's Achala statue also gazed straight ahead. But there is no evidence that Tensei, who was immersed in arduous training and study, gave any thought to the belief that those who possess an Achala statue that gazes forward will found a new school of Buddhism. Perhaps the forward-looking Achala saw to it that, in this case, the legend would come true.

Walking on Fire and Practicing Asceticism

The early months of 1937 were busy for Tensei. Traveling back and forth between Kyoto and Tachikawa, he engaged in Shingon practices at Daigoji toward the Dharma transmission, while in Tachikawa he dedicated himself to offering consultations and performing prayer rites on behalf of those who came for help. All the while he continued to deepen his own Shingon esoteric Buddhist study and practice. In June 1937 he went with Reverend Hokai Urano back to Daigoji, where he was appointed to the lowest priestly rank of *gonrisshi*. That is when he received permission to perform the *kaji* prayer rite from Daigoji. His congregation was also recognized as a branch of Daigoji.

Tensei's effort was arduous. By the end of the summer of 1937 Reverend Urano had transmitted the fire samadhi rite to Tensei. In this ceremony a practitioner walks across live coals or burning wood. The rite is passed down in the Shugendo tradition of mountain asceticism. The term *samadhi* refers to a heightened state of profound meditative concentration. Fire samadhi connotes a state of deep concentration in which Achala burns away and purifies the delusions of all beings with the wisdom of buddhahood manifested in fire. Shugendo ascetics have performed the fire walk since ancient times as part of training to manifest the compassion of Achala.

The burning fire that one sees in the background of traditional images of Achala symbolizes his deeply concentrated compassion that guides all beings to spiritual liberation. The samadhi of Achala is the practice of dwelling in the same state as Achala by turning one's whole body into a flame that burns away the negativity that exists in all sentient beings. It is an esoteric rite that can only be performed when the trainee enters a profound state of meditative interpenetration with fire.

Tensei planned to publicly perform the fire samadhi on September 14, on a plot of land within the courtyard of a shrine situated at the southernmost end of the Tachikawa airfield. The shrine to "the guardian deity for aviators" had been built in 1929 to protect pilots flying in and out of the airport. It was renamed the Shrine of the Sun after the war. Reverend Urano oversaw the event, which was expected to attract a large crowd. The ritual was scheduled to begin at five o'clock that evening, since the audience would be unable to see the flames in full daylight. The morning of the event it began to rain, so Reverend Urano arranged to borrow tents from the elementary and junior high schools to accommodate the spectators.

Green bamboo stalks were erected at the four corners of the space allotted for the rite, with ceremonial ribbons made of straw strung between them. Evergreen branches 1 meter high, adorned with zigzag paper streamers bound with hemp, were planted at the base of each bamboo stalk. An Achala mandala was hung in front of the shrine. Salt was sprinkled on the four sides of the altar to purify it. Pine coals, which were used rather than harder coals because they burned brightly while producing less heat, were spread on the ground. Pine

An aerial view of Tachikawa (c. 1940) with the railway station in the center and the airfield to the north. Photo courtesy of the Tachikawa City Historical Folk Museum.

coals also did not have sharp edges, so women and children were less likely to cut their feet walking over them.

The grounds of the shrine were filled with spectators, including members of Shinjo's old Fifth Regiment, city council members, a local military police unit, a representative from the town office, a group of other veterans, many members of the Fellowship of Light, and members of the public. The coal bales, now empty, were placed at the four corners of the bed of coals and lit. Almost immediately the bed began to burn with bluish white flames, like a rippling sea of fire.

Tensei approached the altar, sat down, and began the rite of Bezaiten, a heavenly Dharma protector and protector of the Byozeisho tradition that had been handed down in his family. As he performed the various stages of the rite he gradually began to enter the profound concentration of samadhi. Once he had entered deeply into the state of concentration, Tensei stood and walked across the bed of flaming coals. With each step his foot sank ankle deep into the coal and the hushed crowd could hear the audible crunch of coals beneath his feet.

Placing one's feet onto burning coals would ordinarily cause severe burns, but Tensei had achieved a state of spiritual resonance with the fire element. As the western sky turned a deep hue of reddish amber, everyone watched Tensei in amazement. Spectators would later remark that the image of Tensei in the twilight forming mudras as he walked across the glowing bed of coals, flickering from the earth still moist from the morning's purifying rainfall, resembled an elaborate scroll painting.

After Tensei had successfully traversed the entire bed of coals, other practitioners were allowed to traverse it. By that time the fire had dimmed and the coals felt warm rather than hot. Walking across was then not much more difficult than walking on a mattress that had been laid out in the summer sun. Tensei later reminisced about the day:

Even children walked amid the flames without a single scratch, crossing with their wooden clogs held in their hands. It is impossible to explain it scientifically. When we cultivate the determination to deliver those around us to a state of awakening through the great, transcendent power of buddhahood, extraordinary, wondrous results will occur, no matter how destructive or negative our past actions may have been. Pursuing the Buddhist path is an exercise in determination. The two characters that make up the Japanese word "determination" mean "awakening" and "enlightenment" on their own. This is a reminder, I think, that we need determination to transform our mindset into one that wants happiness for others as well as for ourselves. When the joy of that pursuit wells up within us, we will begin to experience the wondrous power of the illuminating wisdom, which is the transcendent power of buddhahood.

Tensei was also known to have practiced *tero*, an ascetic practice that involves placing a lit candle on one's inner arm as one meditates. When the candle burns all the way down, it makes a sound as it singes the flesh, extinguishing. Tensei would repeat the practice until he entered deeply into a state of meditative concentration.

In the esoteric Buddhist tradition, ascetic practices like fire walking and tero are methods by which a trainee can transcend strong emotions like bitterness or distress. Such emotions limit one's ability to enter the profound concentration of samadhi and prevent channeling the power of buddhahood to others. These are the most intense examples of Tensei's ascetic practice. "We cannot successfully accomplish these practices while trying to calculate their result," Tensei later told Junna Nakada, who would become the chief abbot of the Daigoji Monastery. "We cannot practice if we are worrying about our own lives."

Tensei's attitude inspired Egen Saeki, who was then the chief abbot of the monastery, to single him out for praise in front of other monks, saying, "A practitioner's attitude should always be like his. You should do your best to follow his example."

I was told that this sort of strict asceticism must always be practiced under the supervision of a master and is not intended for purely lay practitioners.

Building a New Temple

Those who observed Tensei's handling of the fire ritual at the Tachikawa airfield in September 1937 were likely either amazed by his spiritual power or thought it was a trick. Either way, it isn't difficult to imagine that Tensei Ito of the Fellowship of Light quickly became the subject of much talk in Tachikawa and neighboring communities. Until then, Tensei's group was relatively unknown, but his public holding of the ritual helped spread the word and attracted more people to the Fellowship. More than any other single act during that decade, Tensei's September 1937 fire walk caused the population of the Fellowship to swell.

By the end of that summer, Tensei's original group of about thirty had grown to more than two hundred. His house, where the Achala statue was enshrined, had become far too small to accommodate the entire group. Tomoji would later recall that the entrance to their house would be filled with visitors' shoes, and every room packed to capacity. It became almost impossible to find a place to sit.

Tensei moved quickly to expand their residence to accommodate the increasing number of sangha members and dug deep into an already strained family budget to purchase the necessary building materials. Before New Year's Day they added to the house a small corridor that connected to an extra room with a closet. But in January 1938, the landlord, who had previously given his blessing to the expansion, reneged on his promise, bringing the work to a halt.

When Tensei pressed the landlord about his change of heart, he found that other groups in the area who were jealous of the growth of the Fellowship of Light, as well as certain practitioners within the Fellowship who disagreed with the direction Tensei and Tomoji were taking the group, had led a behind-the-scenes effort to stop the expansion of the house. One board member in particular led the opposition, the same member who had pressured Tensei into burying Chibun's remains at a temple in the neighboring city of Akishima as part of a plan to develop a cemetery on temple grounds and personally profit from the proceeds. In this instance he had joined forces with the head priest of a nearby temple, who until this point had always been good to Tensei, to oppose the construction.

Tensei was devastated, and later wrote of his near despair:

> This was almost unbearable for me, and I couldn't keep from crying. If I had been a layperson, I would probably have become angry and sued the landlord or taken the matter to arbitration, but as a person devoted to spiritual practice, I felt I had to follow the principle of nonresistance. Instead of provoking argument, I yielded and accepted the situation. We tore down the extra room that had been added at such expense and effort and humbly asked the congregation to help us by buying the used lumber as firewood. I cannot begin to express my heartfelt gratitude for all those who so selflessly helped us.

No doubt the experience brought to Tensei's mind the often-used phrase "Invite happiness from misfortune." The Fellowship immediately began to discuss a new solution, and two different opinions emerged, both of which had merit.

One group thought it would be best to build a new temple from the ground up, while the other, because of the uncertain economic environment, preferred to keep their options open by renting a large house. They noted that Japan was already on a war footing and thought that the strict rationing that was starting to be imposed would make it difficult to find the necessary materials to build an entirely new structure. The first group believed that since the war effort would cause the price of building materials to continue to rise, construction of a new building should begin as soon as possible. After listening to both groups, Tensei concluded that a new building made the most sense, and the board finally agreed.

The next decision was where to build. Tensei and Tomoji meditated on the question daily, and they settled on a 476-square-meter piece of land in Tachikawa directly to the west of the Suwa Shrine, which was established in 811 as a branch of the main Suwa Shrine in Shinano. The site was isolated from the rest of the town—nothing but mulberry groves as far as the eye could see. Tensei later recalled Tomoji wondering, "If we build a hall in a place like this, will people ever come to visit?" But she also came to believe that "This is the land the buddhas want."

Some of the board members were concerned that no matter what potential they had seen through meditation, the area was much too isolated and inconvenient. They pointed out that north of the railway station was a better choice, as it was prosperous, had homes and

Tensei's sketch and notes that describe the location
of the community's new temple

shops, and was the site of the annual town festival. But Tensei and
Tomoji, after repeated visits to the site, saw more and more potential
in the plot of land that was then a mulberry field. It was no more than
a kilometer west of their residence at Nanko-cho and was near a run-
ning stream from where the gables of the Shinto shrine could be seen.
Tomoji later wrote:

> The place was indeed isolated and a long way from convenient transporta-
> tion, but each time we visited it we were struck by an indescribable feeling
> of purity. We became convinced that this was a site that would be chosen
> by buddhas. We told the other members of our group that even though we
> could not fully comprehend how, it would surely become clear to us in five
> or ten years.

Their conviction would be vindicated sooner than that. Later, as the war intensified, many residents north of the station were evacuated by government order and the buildings almost all destroyed by Allied bombs. Today, Shinnyo-en's main temple complex is still at that same location, which is now about a 10-minute walk from the south side of the Tachikawa railway station.

On March 7, 1938, Tensei leased the land, and on June 8 construction began with a groundbreaking ceremony for divine protection, followed by a topping-out ceremony on August 3 as the building's ridgepole was erected. However, construction did not always proceed smoothly.

The new temple to enshrine Achala under construction in the summer of 1938

Collecting the necessary funds was difficult, and on more than one occasion work had to be suspended. Tensei and Tomoji cut back their expenses even further, and construction was finally completed at the end of September, although only after Tensei borrowed money and sold his last Leica. On October 3 Tensei performed the land purification and consolatory rite, a thousand-year-old ritual Tensei had been intiated into at Daigoji. Three days later, Tensei transported the Achala statue from his home to the newly built temple and performed a homa rite to commemorate its arrival.

Founding the Tachikawa Fellowship of Achala

After being recognized as a branch organization of Daigoji, Tensei was given permission to build a temple for the Tachikawa Fellowship of Achala on July 15, 1938. When Tensei received the document granting permission from Egen Saeki of Daigoji, he wrote the following short poem in his diary:

> With gratitude for the buddhas' loving-kindness,
> insignificant person though I am,
> still I follow the Dharma
> and walk the path with my wife, Tomo.

The poem expresses Tensei's peaceful desire to walk the Buddhist path with Tomoji. Tensei fully understood Tomoji's contributions to their partnership. He always gave her credit as the cofounder of the spiritual community he formed. By writing "Tomo" with the character that means "Dharma friend," he refers to her as not only his wife but also his friend in the Dharma.

Tensei held a homa rite on October 8 to commemorate the founding of the Tachikawa Fellowship of Achala, which later became "Shinchoji" temple, and simultaneously dissolved the Fellowship of Light. The new hall, which would be considerably expanded over the years, initially could hold only a seated group of about fifty people. What's more, limited construction funds caused the roof to leak, so every time it rained Tensei and Tomoji had to pull out more than two dozen tatami mats and lay them out to dry in the sun. But to Tensei, Tomoji, and the growing members of the Tachikawa Fellowship of Achala, the new temple felt like the start of something big.

The budding spiritual community in front of their very first temple, October 3, 1938

Two months later, on December 8, 1938, the ninety-sixth abbot of Daigoji, Egen Saeki, gave Tensei the Dharma name "Kongoin Shinjo." *Shinjo* means "True Vehicle," and *kongo* means "vajra," Sanskrit for both "thunderbolt" and "diamond." Kukai, the founder of Japanese Shingon Buddhism, also had the word *kongo* in the Dharma name he received from his master, Huiguo. So Tensei's Dharma name became Kongoin Shinjo, but he has otherwise been known from then on simply as Shinjo Ito.

III.

SHINJO

9

Attaining Mastery

Using Skillful Means to Bring Dharma to the Masses

A ceremony to officially consecrate the new temple was held on February 5, 1939, and was led by Shinpo Yoshida, an official from the Daigoji Monastery. The formal name of the new facility was the Tachikawa Fellowship of Achala of the Daigo School of Shingon Esoteric Buddhism. In practice, the facility is usually just referred to as "the hall." By any name, the temple was founded as a branch of Daigoji and belonged to the Daigo school of Shingon esoteric Buddhism.

Commemorative photo taken on the day of the consecration ceremony of the Tachikawa Fellowship of Achala, with Shinjo sitting in the center of the front row

Shinjo put up a board outside the temple with the following message:

All who yearn to breathe free from anguish and distress, all who are buffeted by the winds and waves of the stormy voyage through life, come here!

The innermost truths of Shingon esoteric Buddhism are transmitted within this training hall; here we aim to facilitate attainment of peace of mind and a state of calm through the practice of its rituals and prayers.

Consultations
Authentic Spiritual Readings based on:

I Ching

Astrology

Physiognomy

Feng shui

Palmistry

We offer:

Protection from curses, mishaps, and ailments

Private consultation in all matters

Effective means of gaining complete peace of mind and spiritual calm

The board advertising Shinjo's services certainly appealed directly to superstition and folk belief, touting as it did a variety of forms of divination, fortunetelling, and protection from curses. Discriminating denizens of Tokyo, even back then, would have scoffed at its grand promises. Shinjo was aware of how the message would be perceived by some, but he posted it anyway. A few years later he reflected in his diary on the reasons for doing so:

> Orthodox religious groups such as those at Takahata or Mount Takao in this area would not put up a sign like this. They may attract many people, but services and ceremonies alone cannot heal a person's soul.
>
> This sign will surely be cause for ridicule among the "cultured," the so-called intellectuals of society. The more popular my services become, the more what is written on the sign may be used against me. I anticipate this. Yet it does not deter me from posting the sign.
>
> While those taking pride in their sophisticated ways may superficially scoff at us, I know that, in truth, they too need help. I believe religion is for responding to such needs. The day they get what they need—after having come in response to what is written on the sign—they may very well ask me to take it down.

This diary entry brims with Shinjo's determination and reflects his view of religion. Sophisticated, rational, cultured people are likely to dismiss what he wrote as irrational superstition and may even laugh at it. But from Shinjo's point of view, sophistication and rational thinking alone cannot resolve people's suffering. In fact, the opposite is clearly true: suffering persists even for those steeped in culture and rationality. I believe the Buddha rightly said that everyone's life is characterized by the four sufferings of birth, old age, sickness, and death.

For Shinjo, it was evident that although rationality and sophisticated culture may provide pleasant and enriching experiences in life, they do not deal with the reality of our births, the avoidance of aging, the inevitability of falling ill, or the certainty of our deaths. He wanted us to be aware that these are existential realities that we may not consciously realize, but deep in our hearts we are certainly aware of them. Sooner or later we will confront suffering and seek relief. When pain and suffering strike, seemingly without rhyme or reason, the rationality or irrationality of the means to relieve it is no longer of primary concern; we simply search for relief, sometimes in places we normally would not.

No matter how cultured we might be, Shinjo felt, as human beings we all suffer problems that we cannot solve on our own. Shinjo thought that religion was exactly what we need at such times. Even at this early stage of his teaching career, Shinjo sought to adapt his teachings and practice to modernity. For him, that meant not only protecting the tradition that had been passed down from master to disciple, but cultivating a living faith tradition rooted in the lay-person's struggle to live life and be human.

So with great determination, Shinjo hung his sign specifically to speak to those plunged into the depths of suffering. He didn't discourage people from coming to the Fellowship of Achala to solve their problems. In fact, the prayer rites advertised on his sign had a reputation for being quite effective. He was beginning to be known as a priest with a great spiritual capacity, and the Achala enshrined in his temple was rumored to have miraculous powers. These are no doubt the primary reasons that the number of people attending his temple continued to grow.

However, despite his acceptance of the fact that people would turn to his fellowship hoping to solve their personal problems, Shinjo did not intend to become the type of religious leader who espoused that prayer or spiritual powers can solve all of one's problems. The protection that prayer rites provide may help people with mundane problems, but Shinjo knew that getting too caught up in these sorts of workaday miracles and the mystery of spiritual powers would lead one astray from the true purpose of Buddhism, which is liberation from suffering altogether and the attainment of our own buddhahood.

A pithy "three-phrase teaching" summarizes the essential message of the *Mahavairochana Sutra*. When questioned regarding the foundation of all wisdom, Mahavairochana, the personification of cosmic truth itself, says, "Make an attitude of enlightenment the seed, make great compassion the root of your deeds, and complete these with expedient means." In other words, wisdom begins with an aspiration to achieve enlightenment, and its foundation is compassion that seeks to guide all beings out of suffering. Based on wisdom and compassion, ultimately it is to be able to be selfless and see what expedient means are necessary to lead others to enlightenment. Shinjo's appeal to the mundane concerns of ordinary people with his sign embodies this three-phrase teaching.

Keeping Miracles in Perspective

In response to an article on faith healing that appeared in a Shingon journal called *Rokudai*, in May 1940 Shinjo wrote in his diary:

> I for one cannot agree with the idea of relying on the spiritual to treat only illnesses. We must remind ourselves of what is fundamental to the liberation that buddhas aim for: that we sentient beings have the potential and capacity to climb out of states in which we are dominated by inborn animal

instincts. Doing so will help us come within the bounds of true humanity, and from there we can elevate ourselves further and further until we reach the state of enlightenment we find in buddhahood. It may be that mystical experiences of spiritual healing may occur in the process of our religious efforts to elevate ourselves, but any spiritual path that diverges from the primary goal—enlightenment—is, I would say, one that has gone astray.

I can't say that the spiritual therapy introduced in *Rokudai* makes me happy. It sets forth only spiritual healing. [Likewise,] teachings that focus only on physical ailments or on what we can see with our eyes are empty of truth. The Dharma must not be turned into something that is false. I realized this point in reading this article.

For Shinjo, even if esoteric Buddhist rituals heal both spiritual and physical illnesses, that is never their ultimate aim. Healing may occur as we develop the enlightened attitude of bodhichitta (bodhi mind, the aspiration to awaken), but it is only a secondary effect. Incidental healing is not the essence of Shingon Buddhism, nor of any authentic religion for that matter. Shinjo warned that if we get too caught up in these phenomena, we lose sight of the essence of Buddhism.

Shinjo's attitude concerning spiritual powers, whether his own or of others, calls to mind the famous Japanese Buddhist monk Myoe, who lived during the Kamakura period (1185–1333). Myoe was said to have possessed special abilities. He was famously responsible for making it rain after a drought of more than eighty days and became known for his prescience in other matters as well.

Once, in the middle of performing a ritual, Myoe said, "An insect has fallen into the hand-washing basin. Take it out immediately and release it." When his disciple went to look, he found that a bee had fallen into the basin and was on the verge of death.

Another time, in the middle of meditation Myoe said, "A small bird is being attacked in the bamboo grove behind the temple. Go and see." When the disciple went to check, he found a hawk grappling a sparrow, so he chased the hawk away. Such mysterious happenings are said to have occurred so often that Myoe's disciples grew afraid that he could see everything they were doing, and were always careful about how they behaved. People began to consider Myoe a manifestation of the Buddha himself.

But Myoe would have none of it, as indicated in a biography of the monk titled *Toganoo Myoe Shonin Denki*:

> Oh, the things these foolish people say! Instead they ought to take pleasure in meditation and practice the teachings of the Buddha. I never intended to become this way, but after practicing the Dharma for many years I naturally became accomplished without even realizing it. It is nothing to boast about. It is like drinking when you are thirsty or approaching the fire when you want to be warm.

Regarding his own powers, Shinjo clearly agreed with Myoe's attitude. Buddhism teaches that sincere religious training can naturally produce a state of samadhi or profound concentration. Samadhi itself is nothing special; anyone with sufficient training can achieve it. According to Myoe and Shinjo, extraordinary abilities are as ordinary as the impulse to drink when thirsty or to go near a fire when cold. Those who attain samadhi can perform "miracles" related to what Buddhist sutras call the "six supernormal abilities" (*abhijna*):

1. the ability to travel freely anywhere one wishes
2. the ability to see anything anywhere or to foresee the future
3. the ability to hear any sound anywhere
4. the ability to know the minds of others
5. the ability to know past lives
6. the ability to eliminate the delusions at the root of suffering

Of course, these sound fantastical and are far beyond ordinary human capabilities. But such stories about miraculous powers are not unique to Buddhism. Christianity and most other religions preserve in their traditions stories of saints who exhibited similar powers.

Even though Shinjo and Tomoji had spiritual abilities, Shinjo consistently warned against becoming fixated on the supernatural aspects of religion. In fact, he advised his followers that if they were sick, they shouldn't rely on faith alone but should see a doctor. Shinjo may have felt compelled to warn his students because of his own painful experience of losing Chibun. "Practice is not about wanting buddhas to comply with our human desires," Shinjo wrote in his diary.

No religious practitioner is omnipotent. Even the Buddha himself couldn't prevent the destruction of his own relatives. If an esoteric ritual healed a disease, it simply meant that the ritual had been perfectly carried out in accordance with the teachings and practice that are designed to inspire us to seek buddhahood, to arouse the bodhichitta and guide us toward spiritual advancement. Taking up esoteric Buddhist practice simply to heal an illness suggests a faith that serves only oneself and that will produce only self-serving benefits. This type of religious practice has no heart. Getting too caught up in the power of prayer rites to heal illness easily leads us to fall back into a limited, shamanistic conception of practice.

Shinjo and Tomoji at the main gate of the Tachikawa Fellowship of Achala

Undertaking Arduous Training to Receive Transmission

Egen Saeki, an accomplished monk who combined scholarly knowledge with personal virtue, served as Shinjo's primary teacher during
the most arduous portion of his training. Saeki was chief abbot of
Daigoji and had studied Indian philosophy at Tokyo Imperial University (now the University of Tokyo). It was unusual, even unprece-
dented at the time, for a chief abbot to take such a young monk under
his wing. Shinjo greatly respected him.

It was during this period that Shinjo climbed the Kami Daigo
complex in the upper reaches of the mountain monastery to offer
his respects at Kaizando Hall, dedicated to the great master Shobo
Rigen, the founder of the Daigoji Monastery. There, at the peak
of the monastic complex, Shinjo received guidance on how to prepare for the Ein transmission, one of the two lineages passed down
at Daigoji. It is an extremely arduous seven-phase process, at the
end of which a final transmission takes place. The word *kanjo* (Skt.

abhisheka), which we translate here as "transmission," literally means "anointing." It is a process central to esoteric Buddhism, whereby a disciple is empowered by his master to carry out specific esoteric practices. Daigoji is home to another lineage called Diamond and Matrix Realm (Dual Realm) lineage; upon completion of the Dual Realm Dharma transmission, the initiate becomes an *acharya* (master teacher), and is then qualified to start his own lineage.

Even Kukai himself had become a master by undergoing the rite of transmission with his master, Huiguo. Huiguo was the only Buddhist master in China at that time who had received Dharma transmission based on both the *Mahavairochana Sutra* and the *Vajrasekhara Sutra*. He had more than one thousand students. Junna Nakada, the current chief abbot of Daigoji, describes the Dharma transmission as follows in his book *Mienai Kokoro wo Miru* (lit. "looking into the invisible mind"):

> We have an extremely arduous practice passed down directly from the great master Kukai. First, we pay homage to Nyoirin Kannon Bodhisattva (Chintamani Avalokiteshvara). Then we progress through the steps called the Eighteen Paths, the Diamond Realm, the Matrix Realm, and homa. In all, we perform 108 days of practice. At the end of this period, we take part in the Dharma transmission, which connects you to a living lineage all the way back from Mahavairochana down to us today.

Since knowledge of the Dharma transmission rites of esoteric Buddhism are generally not put down in writing but are transmitted individually from master to disciple, it would be inappropriate to describe them in detail. As Junna Nakada explains in his book *Mienai Kokoro wo Miru*:

There is a strict agreement that prohibits people from talking about the contents of the consecration rite with outsiders. In the case of the Dual Realm transmission rites, the agreement is written in extremely difficult language. But it is expressed in simpler words in the Ein tradition: "You must not speak of this matter to even your parents or siblings. If you speak of it to them, your head may explode."

Whether one's head will actually explode or not, the severity of the warning makes clear that the transmissions are meant to be confidential. What should be clear from the above statements is that these rites require intensive preparation, sometimes years of training, and are not lightly undertaken. Such rites form the core of esoteric Buddhism.

Ceremony of completing the Ein transmission with Egen Saeki, chief abbot of Daigoji, in the center, and Shinjo standing behind him, October 1939

Shinjo devoted himself to his effort to prepare for the Ein transmission in 1937 and completed the process under the guidance of Egen Saeki in October 1939. It is remarkable to note that Shinjo was in the middle of the arduous process of completing the Ein transmission when he was also overseeing the construction of the new temple for his group. Shinjo lost a tremendous amount of weight during the process, but was still able to complete the trying program. According to Yushu Okada, the 101st abbot of Daigoji, "It is extremely difficult to complete the Ein transmission unless one is very strong of will and physically healthy." Perhaps the death of his dear son Chibun the year before had strengthened his resolve. Whatever drove him, it is clear that he was resolute in his determination to complete even the most difficult austerities.

Struggling to Train and Lead in Wartime

Japan had plunged into a war with China in 1937. In 1939, Japan became part of a military alliance with Fascist Germany and Italy in pursuit of shared expansionist policies. In 1941, Japan launched a surprise attack on the US military base at Pearl Harbor in Hawaii and declared war on the United States and the United Kingdom.

As early as 1940, international reaction to the expansionist moves of Japan, Germany, and Italy had already led to severe shortages of food and fuel and hardship for the Japanese people. Throughout the war, the Japanese wartime bureaucracy regulated every aspect of daily life, including religion.

By 1941 the Religious Corporations Ordinance, which deemed that all religious activity was subject to state control, had led to the consolidation of all Shingon schools into one. In 1944, the government declared all religious denominations in Japan, including Buddhism, Shinto, and Christianity, to be subsumed under the monolithic rubric of the highly nationalistic State Shinto. It was as though any religious activities other than prayer for military victory and the long life of the emperor would not be tolerated.

Under these conditions, it was difficult to teach Buddhism or to guide people in a truly religious or spiritual context. Shinjo and many other Buddhist monks feared that the Buddhist establishment was losing its way under tightening government control, and because of this, its effectiveness to influence and help people was diminishing. This was of deep concern to Shinjo. In 1940 he wrote in his diary:

> Shingon esoteric Buddhism is a highly mystical form of practice, so at a time like this, if all we do is resort to doctrine, words, and teachings that are difficult for laypeople to understand, will they be persuaded? Theory and reason alone will never help them. But neither will ritual and ceremony alone help them. The Buddha's great vow was to never cease until all beings are liberated from suffering. Unless we act on this vow, people will come to see our doctrine and spiritual tradition as empty.

In late 1941 Shinjo returned to the same sentiments in his diary.

> Those in the Buddhist establishment shamelessly take money from small communities like ours, but all they do is perform rituals and ceremonies. Isn't it precisely this that allows State Shinto to pressure us Buddhists?

Shinjo wanted to guide as many people as possible on the path of buddhahood. He intended to use traditional practice and ritual, but in a way that would transcend simple problem solving or wish fulfillment. Although he was undergoing intense practice at Daigoji, Shinjo knew that this type of training would be impractical for most. Instead, he hoped to lead his students to embrace a Buddhist way of life in a manner that would awaken their mind to life's deeper realities. From his point of view, training was more than correctly practicing rituals or properly chanting words. Training also involved teaching oneself to think differently, training one's mind to awaken like a buddha.

"I will never cease until all beings are liberated from suffering." This is one of the four great vows of a buddha. Shinjo worried that the war's harsh conditions and the government crackdown on religion would make fulfilling this vow particularly challenging. It had been more than five years since he had quit his job as an aircraft engineer to pursue a religious path. Shinjo had become steeped in his own practice and training, and was beginning to come into his own as a teacher and leader of a growing community. We can imagine how he must have worried about war, which gives so little importance to human life and takes away so much. As his young followers were drafted and sent off to battle, he told them, "You must protect the life that the buddhas have given you. Make sure you come home alive."

As the war dragged on, living conditions in Japan worsened. All kinds of supplies and facilities were commandeered for the war effort. Food production declined, causing shortages that led to widespread malnutrition. Most families relied on the black market to survive. A newspaper at the time reported that a public prosecutor who had stubbornly refused to live on anything but rationed food had died of starvation.

Despite the trying circumstances, Shinjo continued his training. On March 5, 1943, he received the complete Dual Realm Dharma transmission from Egen Saeki. Having been initiated into both the Ein lay tradition of Shugendo and the monastic Dual Mandala tradition, he had now become a great master in his own right within the Daigo denomination of Shingon.

While some take little notice of the Ein Transmission, for Shinjo the nonmonastic, the Shugendo tradition was the more important of the two. Although he was a recognized master of monastic practice, even in the 1930s and 1940s, Shinjo maintained the appearance of a layman when interacting with people. Being able to bring the Buddhist path to people on their own level was very important to Shinjo.

Shinjo (*back, fourth from the right*) and other monks receiving the Dual Realm Dharma transmission at Daigoji, March 5, 1943

In November 1944, US B-29s launched an all-out airstrike on Tokyo, and subsequently all over Japan. Bombing raids were particularly acute in cities; most smaller communities like villages were spared this type of carpet bombing. The military establishment had already lost its air command base to US bombs, but because Tachikawa still had an airport, it was often targeted. Large swaths of wooden houses caught fire and were burned in the raids. Many people were left homeless.

At the time, Shinjo and Tomoji had five children. In 1944, their oldest daughter, Eiko, was eleven, Yuichi was seven, Atsuko was four, Masako was two, and their youngest, Shizuko, was a little over a year old. In April 1945, Tomoji and the children evacuated to Yamanashi, joining many other city dwellers who had taken refuge in smaller towns and villages.

Under these conditions, Shinjo's religious activities were of course interrupted. Whenever he returned from visiting his family in the countryside, he would bring back precious food to distribute among the people who flocked to his temple. As food rationing continued even after the Japanese surrender, for a period after the war he used the land surrounding the temple to grow sweet potatoes and pumpkin squash. He personally dug holes in the ground to store the potatoes, and he stacked the squash in the garden for distribution to his congregants. Even a handful of rice or wheat or a single potato was a precious commodity during those dire times.

Rising in the Ranks at Daigoji

Even during such difficult times, Shinjo was making a name for himself among the Daigoji hierarchy. Although his temple was small, because he was a direct disciple of Egen Saeki, his ko, now called Fellowship of Achala, was removed from the jurisdiction of the main administrative branch office in eastern Japan and placed directly under the jurisdiction of the denomination's central headquarters at Daigoji. Then in 1941, two years after Shinjo received the Ein transmission, Daigoji appointed Shinjo acting head priest of the venerable temple Johoin.

Johoin is in Musashi Murayama, a city northwest of Tachikawa. It is a large, historic temple affiliated with the Shugendo lineage at Daigoji. Its grounds cover a terrain of about 6.6 square kilometers. The previous head priest of Johoin had been ill, and by the time Shinjo was appointed to the post it had become a wild, almost desolate place.

Photo of Johoin in the town of Musashi Murayama

When he was named acting head priest of Johoin, Shinjo was also promoted from the rank of *risshi*, which he had attained the previous year, to that of *gonshosozu*, and then to *shosozu*. During his tenure as acting head priest, Shinjo successfully renovated Johoin. When the renovated temple was reconsecrated and returned to Daigoji's direct administration in 1946, Shinjo felt he could resign from his post as acting head priest. This progression of events suggests that although he was still a young man, his dedicated efforts had impressed the administration of Daigoji and they expected great things from him.

10

Becoming Independent

Branching Off from Daigoji to Found the Sangha of Truth

On August 15, 1945, Japan surrendered unconditionally to the Allied powers and the Pacific War ended. On December 28 the Religious Corporations Ordinance was enacted, guaranteeing freedom of religion. The single unified Shingon denomination that had absorbed all the various subschools was dismantled, and Shinjo's home monastery of Daigoji once again became the independent headquarters of the Daigo school of Shingon Buddhism.

Shinjo chose not to continue the Fellowship of Achala's affiliation with the Daigoji Monastery. Shinjo was forty-two. Just as he had once taken a risk by quitting his job and dedicating himself full-time to his religious vocation, once again he eschewed the safe and easy path. This time, he branched off from his mother temple to create a unique path that was a combination of lay and monastic practices that Shinjo felt would be better suited to helping ordinary people face the practical challenges of life and walk the path to true awakening. With this, Shinjo took a giant step toward addressing a question that had been on his mind as a Buddhist teacher for a long time: How can we lead our followers onto the path to buddhahood if we aren't willing to invite them to become capable, practicing Buddhists themselves?

By 1948, under the tutelage of Egen Saeki, Shinjo Ito had mastered both the Shugendo and Shingon traditions and had completed both the Ein and Dual Mandala Dharma transmissions. Completion of the latter initiation meant that he was recognized as a master capable of conducting Dharma transmission for his own disciples. Shinjo was also qualified to pass on the "Dharma light" of Shingon esoteric Buddhism to those who had attained an appropriately advanced level of training. Assuming the authority he had earned through years of arduous training, on January 23, 1948, he changed the name of his temple to "Shinchoji" (temple of truth and clarity) and reformed his religious organization under the new name "Sangha of Truth" (Makoto Kyodan)—the direct precursor to Shinnyo-en.

We may wonder, if the new community was like traditional Shingon, why did Shinjo feel it necessary to make the bold move toward independence? Reflecting on Shinjo's spiritual evolution, we see a clear progression leading to this change. From a young age Shinjo had inherited a seriousness of purpose and spirituality from his parents. In his young adulthood, he resigned a prestigious job to free himself from obstacles to his practice so he could pursue spiritual mastery in order to display the light of Dharma to the world. During the early period of his life as a religious leader and throughout the war, he struggled to determine how best to guide the members of his Fellowship of Light, most of whom were lay practitioners.

Across all of these formative years, Shinjo continued to search for a form of practice that would offer a more substantive personal transformation than the spiritual faith healing that was common in Japan at the time. Shinjo had been looking for a way to enable people to look beyond their immediate worries to see themselves at a deeper level, with the goal of becoming more spiritually awakened. He knew that he couldn't expect his community of lay practitioners with jobs and families to commit to even the most basic structures of monastic training. Shinjo was intent on building a modern practice that would allow people to find the buddha within themselves.

Being true to one's own buddhaness or awakenedness was very important to Shinjo. So he chose to call his reformed community "Sangha of Truth" to emphasize the central role of being truthful to our own innate awakenedness in word and deed as we pursue the path. In a diary entry he wrote:

Shinjo at the altar room of Shinchoji, October 1948

The word "truth" (*makoto*) refers to truth as it always is. It refers to awakening to know what is a matter of fact as a matter of fact. In other words, truth refers to awakening.

Shinjo chose the word "sangha" to concretely express his desire that his disciples envision the new group as an intentional community for people who truly sought buddhahood, and not merely a group that one could turn to for ritual aid in times of immediate need.

In most ways, the newly inaugurated Sangha of Truth was a continuation of the Tachikawa Fellowship of Achala. The rituals and training that Shinjo provided did not dramatically change: he still taught an esoteric Buddhism focused on Achala as a manifestation of the buddha figure Mahavairochana. The 1948 *Kyoto Gongyo Hen* (Chanting Book for General Practitioners) opens with the Threefold Refuge written in both Japanese and Pali and includes passages from the *Achala Sutra* and the *Heart Sutra*, the "Universal Gateway of the Bodhisattva Kanzeon" chapter from the *Lotus Sutra* translated into Japanese, and a set of mantras for recitation. These are all standard Shingon chants. A list of "Guidelines for the Sangha of Truth" published a year later further attests to the traditional program of study and training followed by the Sangha of Truth:

- receive basic precepts
- train in stages toward Dharma transmission
- receive more advanced precepts
- complete the stages of training
- receive Dharma transmission

The fifteen priestly ranks attainable within the Sangha of Truth were also identical to those within the traditional Shingon system.

October 1948 marked the tenth anniversary of the founding of Shinchoji. That month a three-day festival was held to commemorate the occasion. The first two days of the festival featured common Buddhist ceremonies, and the third day featured an outdoor homa rite. Shinjo, dressed as the officiant in a vermillion surplice decorated with round vermillion tassels unique to the Shugendo tradition, entered the homa site at the end of a procession headed by a group of children in ceremonial robes and accompanied by traditional music. It was the first large event held within the community and attracted members from all over the country. The image of the temple overflowing with people symbolized a new beginning for Shinjo and his community.

Shinjo performing an outdoor homa rite to commemorate the tenth anniversary of Shinchoji's establishment, October 5, 1948

The community established the Dharma school Chisenryo (later called Chiryu Gakuin, meaning "wisdom-stream school") to train practitioners to be priests who would teach within the community at Shinchoji and at other affiliated temples, including Mitsugonin, Itokuji in Chiba Prefecture, and Ayumizaki Kannon, also called Chozenji, in Ibaraki Prefecture. The Sangha of Truth went through a period of rapid growth. In the social turmoil that followed the war, a younger generation of practitioners emerged, ushering in a new era for the sangha. These younger members formed a youth cultural association, which held study meetings every Sunday and began publishing *Getsurin*, meaning "moon disc." Soon membership in the Sangha of Truth had swelled to more than fifty thousand.

Taking a Unique Approach to the Path

Nowadays we associate the Japanese word *zen* with Zen Buddhism and its practice of zazen, or sitting meditation. Zen is a Japanese transliteration of the Sanskrit word *dhyana*, which means "meditation" or meditative absorption. The practice of meditation is meant to help people enter a deep state of contemplation by quieting the mind and concentrating it on a single object. This kind of meditative absorption is a basic practice in all forms of Buddhism.

Zen Buddhism emphasizes the practice of meditative concentration, but the practice is by no means limited to Zen Buddhism. In the esoteric Buddhist tradition, monks employ the "three activities" of body, speech, and mind to enter a profound state of resonance and oneness with a particular buddha, in which their minds merge with that particular archetypal buddha. This type of meditative absorption, wherein the practitioner and the buddha intermingle so as to bring to fruition the buddha qualities latent in the practitioner, also makes use of profound meditative concentration.

In most cases, one must undertake strict monastic training to be able to successfully perform this type of practice. It is nearly impossible to reach a deep state of meditative absorption without fully committing to monastic discipline. Having completed the training and become a master himself, Shinjo was intent on leading his lay disciples to the state of spiritual awakening he had attained with such practices. To achieve his aim, he would have to create a new mode of Buddhist practice different from what existed at the time. He wanted to help people acknowledge, by deeply and objectively looking into themselves, that they were innately good and pure. If people could see that they were intrinsically pure, he reasoned, they could then more easily learn to wipe away the fog that obscures the mind. In this way, people would be able to transform their everyday realities into a meaningful Buddhist practice capable of bringing lasting clarity and

Shinjo and Tomoji in front of Shinchoji with
a plaque reading "Sangha of Truth" (1949)

joy. Shinjo's thinking along these lines made up the ideas at the heart of the Sangha of Truth.

In a diary entry from this period, Shinjo ties together the ideas of total sincerity in word and deed in pursuit of awakening and the need for meditation to accomplish it:

> When we get caught up in the tiny bubble of the world centered on our-selves, we fail to understand our daily acts for what they really are. There are some who reflect on themselves enough to see when they are at fault. Then there are those who can do the same when someone points out what they need to see. Then there are those who by disposition are unable to readily accept the word or sound judgment of others.
>
> A mirror, however, always reflects what appears to it. If it becomes clouded or tarnished, we need only to polish it for it to correctly function again. Our hearts and minds are also like a mirror. We want to keep them polished.

The reality of our lives can be perceived as a matter of natural fact. But this is only possible, Shinjo thought, when we are not pre-occupied with ourselves. Just because we have awakened to the truth once doesn't necessarily mean that we will remain awake to it. We easily lose sight of such truth when the mind is clouded. So it is nec-essary to constantly polish and cleanse our minds with meditation. Shinjo writes further:

> Just as a clouded mirror loses its value, if the state of our mind is clouded, obscured by clouds of delusion, its true nature (*shinnyo*) will be unable to shine through. "True nature" is "buddha nature"—the "inner mirror" with

which everyone is equipped. When we polish this inner mirror, our buddha nature or true nature, it shines forth as the truth (*makoto*) of things.

Buddhism begins and ends with awakening. It is ultimately about "the light of one's mind or heart," so to speak. A mind bent on awakening is one bent on polishing the inner mirror. It is thus the mind or heart that prompts one to work diligently to manifest the truth of things or its own true nature.

Shinjo believed that Buddhism began with the Buddha's quest for spiritual awakening and that anyone who steadily walks the same path has the potential to become a buddha, too. If people can become aware of their own buddha nature and work on cultivating it, then they will

Shinjo and Tomoji with students of Chisenryo, March 19, 1949

also start to sense the *shinnyo* (intrinsic nature) of all existence. The realm of enlightenment, he believed, is available to everyone.

Shinjo's thoughts here owe much to views expressed by Kakuban. Shinjo practiced and wrote about one of the fundamental Shingon practices connected to Kakuban called "Full Moon Visualization." In this practice, the meditator clearly visualizes a full moon and, through the visualization, grasps that the mind is innately pure and complete like the full moon. Kakuban articulated the aspects of mind that are to be grasped in the visualization as follows:

> Just as the full moon is pure, I am essentially without tarnish.
> Just as the full moon is round and perfect, I lack nothing.
> Just as the full moon is clear, I am essentially untarnished Dharma.

For Shinjo, Buddhism is the practice of looking at the originally pure mind, our buddha nature, and polishing it in order to realize shinnyo (the innate goodness and the true nature of all things), the enlightenment that Shakyamuni Buddha revealed in his Dharma. His way of thinking does not focus on questions about life after death or the world to come. In this sense, Shinjo's approach embodies Kukai's teachings that focus on "attaining enlightenment in this very body." His thought about enlightenment and the process of reaching it also share some fundamental elements with the thought of the Soto Zen founder Dogen and the thought of Myoe, the patriarch known as the restorer of the Kegon denomination. So although Shinjo's approach was unique to his time and place, his line of thought was also grounded squarely in the long and venerable Japanese Buddhist tradition.

Developing a New Form of Meditative Practice: Sesshin

Over a period of years Shinjo began to develop a system of meditative practice that would be tailored to allow his lay disciples to encounter and polish the innately pure nature of their own minds. From nearly the beginning of the process of development, he used the term *sesshin*, borrowed from the Zen tradition, to refer to his style of practice. In the Zen tradition, sesshin is a period of intensive sitting meditation undertaken in a Zen monastery. The term literally means "touching the heart or mind," and is written with two Chinese characters that mean "to touch" and "heart/mind." In an alternate rendering, the first character is replaced with another one that means "to settle" or "to gather."

Shinjo didn't develop his version of sesshin in a vacuum. Although he was principally a practitioner of Shingon Buddhism, he had a deep respect for Buddhist masters of other denominations. For example, in 1948, Shinjo published a Dharma talk in which he makes clear that he considers his own teachings to be in harmony with the teachings of Dogen in *Getsurin*:

> In his memoirs, Zen Master Dogen wrote that his Master said, "The practice of sitting meditation leads to casting off body-mind. When we engage single-mindedly in sitting meditation, we let go of the five desires and rid ourselves of the five hindrances."
>
> "Casting off" or "sloughing off body-mind" is a state free of delusions,

and sitting meditation produces it. "The five desires" are excessive desire for money, sexual activity, food and drink, fame and fortune, and sleep. The five hindrances are greed, anger, crying over spilled milk, doubt, and sleepiness. Again, "casting off body-mind" is a state that is free of delusions.

Our practice of applying what we realize in meditation at the temple to our daily lives is deeply tied to the spirit of Zen. The sesshin meditative training conducted at the Sangha of Truth—what so many have been referring to as "prayer practice"—is entirely what Zen sitting meditation is about. We earnestly and wholeheartedly contemplate the loving-kindness and compassion of buddhahood with the goal of attaining a state wherein we can cast off body-mind.

Shinjo's deep respect for Dogen may go back to the youthful days when he practiced Zen meditation with his father, a devotee of Soto Zen who served as a community representative at a local Zen temple. His personal experiences with Zen practice may have helped him to find an essential common ground between the seemingly very different practices of Zen and Shingon esoteric Buddhism.

Shinjo's adaptation of sesshin was designed to make it possible for lay practitioners to experience the same meditative absorption typically only available to monastics who undertook intensive training. A unique element that Shinjo introduced in his version of sesshin was the idea that practitioners would be able to objectively encounter their subjective selves "when the individual soul is reflected in the mirror of a spiritual guide."

A spiritual guide would practice together with lay practitioners to help them more easily gain access to states of deep meditation and reflection. The spiritual guide would enter into a state of resonant oneness with a buddha, like Achala for example, as practiced in esoteric Buddhism, and then function as a kind of "mirror" for the lay meditator engaging in the practice.

Ordinarily one becomes able to see one's subjective self objectively only after a long and arduous process of monastic training. But Shinjo made it possible for lay practitioners to experience this as well through the addition of a buddha. The relationship of a buddha to a ritual petitioner via a ritual agent in the form of a practitioner-priest is quite well known in Shingon esoteric Buddhism. Shinjo simply adapted this structure to the practice of sitting meditation so that the buddha might facilitate the state of meditation via the spiritual guide. In this way we can understand Shinjo's version of sesshin as a unique form of esoteric Buddhist meditation.

Sesshin quickly became the signature practice of the Sangha of Truth. Its growing popularity presented a significant challenge to the group during those early years: Where would they find enough spiritual guides capable of entering the profound state of resonant oneness necessary to act as a spiritual mirror for others to serve the burgeoning community? Shinjo and his wife, Tomoji, certainly had the spiritual capacity to do so, but the two of them alone would never be able to address the needs of the thousands of members of the Sangha of Truth.

Eventually, several of Shinjo's disciples who had become live-in disciples toward the end of the war were able to undertake the intensive practice and training needed to attain the ability to act as a spiritual mirrors for others. Their abilities at the time were limited to aiding others in sesshin, whereas Shinjo was capable of performing complex rites on behalf of others. Nevertheless, as more and more of his disciples gradually undertook serious training, the problem was resolved.

As he refined his teaching of sesshin, Shinjo came to think of sesshin as having both a structured and an unstructured aspect.

Structured sesshin refers to the formal practice of sitting meditation undertaken at the temple, whereas unstructured sesshin occurs naturally at any time and any place. To engage in unstructured sesshin means to be more contemplative in daily life to realize opportunities to put into action what one acquires in structured sesshin.

We can also think of "structured" as referring to the tangible, phenomenal world, and "unstructured" as referring to the truth that lies beyond the phenomenal realm. Shinjo would say that the structured sesshin practiced by the Sangha of Truth was equivalent to formal sitting meditation in the Zen denomination, while the "formless" unstructured practice was like the spirit of Zen in which mindfulness in the present moment and observing what is happening without attachment become one's primary practice. In an article titled "The Essential Principles of Makoto Training," he wrote:

> We are not truly practicing Makoto Training if we separate structured sesshin from unstructured practice. Our place of training is in society. That is where we can cultivate ourselves.

In other words, the structured sesshin experienced at the temple is only complete when practiced together with unstructured sesshin, the point of which is to see each of life's activities as a potential opportunity to awaken. Unstructured sesshin uses the insights gained in structured sesshin to put Buddhist ideals into practice in every moment of one's daily life.

Shinjo saw no difference between Shinchoji and a member's home, school, or place of work when it came to practice. Esoteric Buddhism teaches that dharma manifests in all things in the universe. As long as we are willing we can see every aspect of our daily lives as opportunities to train and cultivate enlightenment. Shinjo developed his version of sesshin based on principles of esoteric Buddhism to achieve precisely this.

As Kakuban said, we are essentially without tarnish—we all have the potential to attain enlightenment and liberation, not just a handful of monks and nuns. The practice of sesshin that Shinjo developed helps people to strike a balance between structured, spiritual-guide-mediated practice and a personal form of practice in everyday life. Sesshin is also designed to gently move lay practitioners away from a self-interested type of pursuit that fulfills only the immediate needs to a practice that benefits others as well.

Thus, sesshin was Shinjo's answer to the key questions that had bothered him during the war—how to lead the members of his temple onto a proper Buddhist path and what kind of practice they could do within the framework of the Shingon tradition. The Sangha of Truth, with Shinchoji as its head temple, was basically a traditional esoteric Buddhist group in which ordained clergy preached and performed rituals. But with the new practice of sesshin, he now had the means to help both lay practitioners and ordained clergy alike along the path to awakening and liberation. This formation of a large community of lay practitioners upon the solid foundation of monastic tradition centered around the practice of sesshin was the genesis of what we now know as Shinnyo-en.

Remaining Humble and Growing Spiritually as a Family

During this period of growth and development, Shinjo came to be referred to as "His Eminence the Chief Abbot," or just "His Eminence," according to Japanese Buddhist custom at the time. Yet he remained freely available and eminently approachable to his students. An episode described in the magazine *Getsurin* published at the time tells us something about his character. This occurred shortly before the community's tenth anniversary celebration festival.

Late one night, just after midnight, Shinjo was on the last train of the day on his way home from the nearby branch temple, Hachiyoin. A man he had never seen before, who said he lived near Kichijoji, had fallen asleep, missed his stop, and ended up riding all the way to Tachikawa. It was raining and the man had nowhere to sleep, so Shinjo invited him to spend the night at his home.

"Hello!" Shinjo called out to Tomoji when they arrived. "I've brought a guest!" To the man he said, "Please come in! You see, my home is a temple."

Tomoji came out to greet them, no doubt wondering, "If it's a guest who has come to visit us, surely he already knows this is a temple." But when she understood the situation, she welcomed the stranger, warmed up the room, boiled water, and offered him a cup of tea. It was after 3:00 in the morning before they finally went to sleep. Obviously it was inconvenient for Tomoji to be awake at that hour, since in those days practitioners who volunteered to clean the temple as part of their spiritual training normally arrived at 5:30 in the morning. But this kind of behavior was characteristic of Shinjo and Tomoji. The Shinchoji temple was constructed in the typical style of a Shugendo temple of the early Showa period: the rooms used for religious purposes doubled as living quarters for Shinjo, Tomoji, and their children. Although Shinjo was uncompromising, both as a teacher and practitioner, the community had a family-like atmosphere.

During the time of the Sangha of Truth, and later with Shinnyo-en, this relaxed atmosphere owed much to the openness and the growing stature of Tomoji, who was also becoming a learned practitioner in her own right. In 1949 Shinjo finished creating a program for future holders of his lineage that combined the Shugendo practice of Ein transmission and the Shingon practice of Diamond and Matrix Realm transmission. In 1950, Tomoji became the first person to matriculate through the program, which made her eligible to be the spiritual head of the sangha. With this, the spiritual abilities she had inherited from her grandmother were firmly grounded

Tomoji supporting a homa rite as a ceremonial assistant

within the system of esoteric Buddhism, and she too reached a level of training that corresponded with that of "master" in esoteric Buddhism. Thus, Tomoji became Shinjo's successor in the Dharma lineage.

Everything appeared to be going smoothly for Shinjo and Tomoji, at least professionally, as the Sangha of Truth was gaining momentum at an impressive pace. Still, daily life was difficult. In the years after the Second World War the Japanese population experienced serious hardships, and Shinjo and his family were no exception. In a diary entry from May 1949, Shinjo writes:

> A Family Supper
>
> We may be penniless, but my wife, children, and I are grateful to receive nourishment that allows us to practice. Tonight, we give thanks to our meal: bread and milk with a nip of sugar sprinkled in it—a rare treat. It made me reflect: "Have I, in word and deed, acted in a way that merited our daily bread, this meal of milk with sugar? Have I helped anyone—even one person—today, so that they were able to elevate themselves to embody the teachings with *their* actions?"

Sugar was expensive, but a dinner of bread and milk mixed with a little sugar was certainly no luxury for an ordinary person. Shinjo received his dinner with gratitude, and reflected on whether he had been able to carry out actions worthy of the humble food he ate. He was poor, but in his religious life each day was fulfilling.

Unbeknown to Shinjo and Tomoji, however, they were about to be confronted with some of the most difficult years of their lives.

Tested by Crisis and Loss

Being Accused of a Crime and Publicly Reviled

Late on the night of August 20, 1950, the police were waiting for Shinjo near his temple as he returned from central Tokyo. When he arrived he was promptly placed under arrest. A former disciple of Shinjo's had accused him of using physical violence against him as part of religious training. Tokyo newspapers and radio stations picked up the story and widely reported the accusation, which came to be known as the "Sangha of Truth Incident." Within the community the incident has come to be referred to as the "Dharma Crisis."

The accuser, only twenty-five years old at the time of Shinjo's arrest, had once been Shinjo's apprentice. A promising student, he had been put in charge of religious affairs, a position second only to that of Shinjo, at the age of twenty-three. Shinjo had also put him in charge of the Chiryu Gakuin, the sangha's Dharma school that specializes in the study of doctrine and ritual and trains the sangha's future leaders. He held a position of tremendous power within the sangha. It is only natural that everyone expected that in time he would become the head of the sangha.

Unfortunately, the position this young man had been given and the power that came with it turned out to be too much for him. By the spring of 1949, members within the community became aware that the man had been breaking the Buddhist precepts that any leader of a Dharma community was expected to uphold. He grew negligent in his training and had an inappropriate relationship with a female practitioner. Over a period of months, Shinjo had to frequently caution and admonish this disciple, until he resigned his post and left the sangha in the fall of 1949. It was clear that he felt bitter about the way things had gone.

Shinjo could not help but feel deeply disappointed by what had occurred. The man had been much more than just a disciple. When he was only sixteen, his father had died. Shinjo and Tomoji had taken him into their home and had personally overseen his Buddhist training. Their daughter Masako, now Shinso Ito, considered the man to be like an elder brother. Despite his prior connection and close relationship with the Ito family, in 1950 he filed formal charges against Shinjo and the Sangha of Truth.

The primary charge that the young man levied was that he had been assaulted during a sesshin meditative training. At the time sesshin had not yet evolved into the calm, quiet style familiar to practitioners today. The practice required great effort and fortitude. At times the instructor would tap trainees on the shoulder, or on the back, to encourage them to meditate deeply. At Zen temples there is the traditional practice of striking the shoulders of meditators with a flat wooden stick called a *keisaku* to encourage deeper meditation. What happened at Shinchoji was for a similar purpose, but done with a lot less force and without the stick. The former disciple greatly exaggerated what had occurred during the training, accusing the sangha of torture.

Japan was still passing through a period of social confusion following the war. During this period there was a great surge in the number of so-called new religions, many of which were opportunistic and fraudulent in nature. Despite having cultivated his community for almost fifteen years, Shinjo and the Sangha of Truth were lumped in with all the others in the court of public opinion, which tended to brand all new groups as false. Given this environment, the media had little interest in listening to Shinjo's side of the story. Newspapers ran misleading and sensational accounts of the situation, and the Sangha of Truth was publicly ridiculed and condemned.

Shinjo's situation was almost certainly made worse by the fact that he had recently made his group independent of Daigoji. Unable to rely on his association with Daigoji, a long-established institution of mainstream Japanese Buddhism, people unfamiliar with the Sangha of Truth only saw it as a dangerous new religion. Speaking about the period, Shinjo noted that the townspeople of Tachikawa were clannish, and that the members of Shinjo's sangha were treated as outsiders and denounced as a newly risen cult. There was a period when crowds of people would gather outside Shinchoji, throwing rocks and shouting insults.

Shinjo and Tomoji's son, Yuichi, was thirteen, their daughter Masako was eight, and their youngest daughter, Shizuko, was seven. It was a difficult time for all of them. Yuichi had been ill since the previous year with caries of the hip, a condition that left him walking with crutches. Some of his classmates and other children from his school already made fun of him because of his bad leg, and he suffered even more when they found out about the accusations against his father. Yuichi begged his mother not to make him go to school, telling her that everyone mocked him. Tomoji took him to the altar room and they prayed and meditated together.

After sitting with him for some time, Tomoji spoke to him with tears in her eyes, "Yuichi, if your father hears that you are not going to school, he will be really sad. He's already going through so much. You wouldn't want to cause him any more worries, would you? If you think only about yourself and give in to something like this, you won't be able to follow in your father's footsteps."

Yuichi continued to cry for a while, then said he understood and got to his feet. He never complained again. He continued to go to school, protecting his younger sisters from the stones that came flying at them as they walked through Suwa Park. His sister Masako explained:

> Even though he had to walk with crutches, he would shelter us from the
> stones hurled at us as we made our way to school through the nearby
> woods. Our schoolmates called us "the criminal's children," threw stones
> at us, and pushed us down in the mud. But we gritted our teeth and perse-
> vered, always believing in the Buddha's way.

Yuichi and Masako

Shinjo later wrote, "I wasn't the only one who had to endure ridicule. My children, too, were subject to disparaging remarks and abuse. Sometimes on their way to school, other children threw stones at them. I still remember occasions when they would snatch away Yuichi's crutches, teasing him about his disabled leg."

Turning Hardship into the Path: The Dharma Crisis

After the district police arrested Shinjo on August 20, he was first detained at the local police station before being transferred to Hachioji Prison, where he was kept in a dark, hot cell for forty days. He maintained a positive frame of mind, however, and later recalled, "I spoke to everyone, without distinguishing among them, about the spirit of a buddha. That was my greatest pleasure." In jail the other prisoners mocked Shinjo for his religious devotion, but also grew to respect him. In *The Light in Each Moment* Shinjo recalled one particularly memorable case of a murderer who had killed a member of his family:

> During my imprisonment, I shared a cell with a man who was convicted of the brutal crime of murdering a family member. No one would come close to him, but the prison authorities placed us together, saying, "If you are a man of religion, you should be able to help him."
>
> The man had been badly beaten. His body was covered with scars and he groaned in pain. Broken in body and spirit, at first he tried to attack me as well. However, he gradually became less aggressive as I looked after his wounds. I would cool his forehead with a damp towel soaked in water— a precious item, since we were given little of it in jail—while chanting the

Goreiju. His pain seemed to gradually diminish, and he eventually regained his presence of mind. Another prisoner, who had been watching these events as they transpired, rolled up his sleeve to the shoulder to reveal a poem tattooed to his arm that read:

> It is when we are brought to ruin
> and our sleeves are soaked in tears
> that we see what lies
> in the depths of people's hearts.

He may have just wanted to show off his tattoo, but at the same time I thought he also wanted to share his sorrow for the tragedies that had befallen his life and led to our present situations.

I offered consolatory prayers for my cellmate's victim, and earnestly tried to convey the Dharma to the offender. Perhaps owing to the merit accrued by consolatory prayers offered in the spirit of not distinguishing between friend or foe, my cellmate regained his senses, and with them the desire to repent for the crime he had committed. With my help, he began regularly placing his palms together in *gassho* to the buddhas. When I saw these changes in him, brought about by the great spiritual powers of the buddhas, I was unable to contain my tears of joy. Experiences like that are what is so compelling about religious life, and *when one awakens to it, therein lies true joy.*

Meanwhile, the Sangha of Truth community was on the verge of ruin. "What worried us was that this affair would destroy the sangha," recalled Kashitaro Ide, who was part of Shinjo's defense team. In Shinjo's absence, it fell to Tomoji to hold the community together. She reassured the heads of the community's affiliated temples: "We have to think about the worst-case scenario: that they may confiscate the temple buildings. We are sorry about this young man's betrayal and how far things have gone as a result. If the worst should occur, we will make it up to all of you, even if it means constructing one new building every year to replace the home each of you have lost." Tomoji also spoke to the members of the sangha. "Even if our community is forced to dissolve," she told them, "we will just be returning to where we started. So don't worry. If we must, my husband and I will begin all over again, even without a proper temple." Her words had a calming effect and mitigated the feelings of shock that had spread within the sangha.

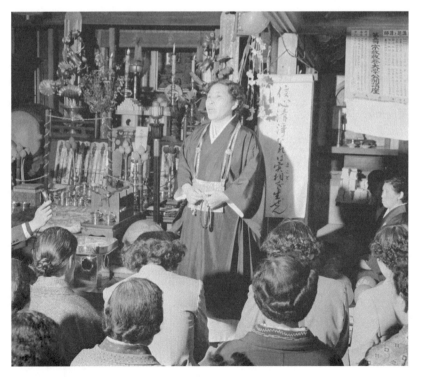

Tomoji talking to sangha members at Shinchoji temple after overcoming the Dharma Crisis, April 8, 1954

Although the very public accusation against Shinjo presented a real threat to the future of the Sangha of Truth, Shinjo did have public supporters as well. The most prominent of these was Ken Kitamura, a successful businessman who had launched Hakuryukaku, or "Fellowship of White Dragons," an independent center for spiritual research. In an issue of the research center's newsletter called *Reiko*, Kitamura defended Shinjo. He wrote that although members of both the media and the public had accused the Sangha of Truth of being a "new" religion, the Sangha of Truth was pure Buddhism. During the crisis Shinjo was forced to suspend publication of the newsletters that the Sangha of Truth had begun to publish. Mr. Kitamura offered *Reiko* as a substitute, and in its pages published news and articles about the case that were sympathetic to Shinjo. He wrote that the affair was not based on fact and that the former disciple's accusation was nothing more than a false charge. "We believe without the slightest doubt that Master Shinjo is completely innocent of all charges," Kitamura wrote.

Shinjo was released from jail on September 26. His daughter Masako described the day:

> In time, our father came home from prison. Everyone cried, even Father and Mother. But Father said to us, "It's all right now. I've come back to you, so there is nothing more to worry about. I know how hard it has been for you. You have been such good children." He then patted each of us on the head. I remember how big and warm his hand was.

Shinjo had only been released on bail, however, and the danger to the community was not yet over. Before his arrest, the hall of Shinchoji, and even the surrounding grounds, had always been filled to capacity. But when the incident broke, many members left the sangha and attendance at Shinchoji began to ebb. Some worried that the Sangha of Truth would no longer be recognized as a religious corporation under the 1951 renewal of the postwar Religious Corporations Act and would be forced to disband.

Although Shinjo's trial did not officially conclude for another four years until it reached the Tokyo High Court, a turning point came in January 1951 when the chief witness for the prosecution took the stand. The man had earlier testified that physical abuse had occurred, but on the stand he recanted, admitting that the police had threatened to keep him in custody indefinitely unless he perjured himself. He blamed the entire situation on religious oppression and the personal grudge of one individual. This created an uproar in the courtroom. After that, the chairman of the local governmental Human Rights Protection Committee began to attend the hearings regularly, and the trial could proceed in a more balanced way. Finally, evidence was presented that Shinjo himself had not been present on the occasion when the accuser had claimed to have been physically abused. Whatever may have happened did not involve Shinjo. After these revelations, the situation for Shinjo and the Sangha of Truth gradually began to improve.

Suffering the Unbearable Loss of a Second Child

As Shinjo's case dragged on in the courts, he and Tomoji were forced to face even greater adversity. Yuichi, their second son, who was born the year after their beloved Chibun's death, had been frail since birth. But Yuichi had not been too fragile to lead an active life. Despite his age and physical condition, he displayed his own special gifts, becoming a spiritual guide for practitioners in the sangha at the age of ten. At fifteen, he observed:

> A candle offers itself to give light to people.
> Buddhas share all your suffering and all your joy.
> It is all right if I don't get well.
> Seeing even one more person freed from
> suffering is what makes me happiest.

In 1949, when Yuichi was eleven, he was admitted to Juntendo Hospital with bone tuberculosis of the hipbone. From that point on he walked only with crutches. The Dharma Crisis occurred in August of the following year, and Yuichi had to attend school while enduring bullying from his schoolmates. By that time he had almost recovered from his illness, but it soon returned, triggered by a simple cold. Yuichi had to be hospitalized again in July 1951.

Yuichi had to endure not only the pain of his illness but also painful treatments, including spinal injections and the injection of nee-

Yuichi before his second hospitalization

dles into his heart to remove excess fluid. But Yuichi was a remarkable young man. "If I think the injections hurt, it means I don't yet have enough gratitude," he told the nurses at Juntendo Hospital. One day he made everyone laugh when he joked, "I've had so many different illnesses, the only kind of doctor I've never been to is a gynecologist!"

Shinjo's time-consuming legal problems made it difficult for him to spend much time with his critically ill son. Not only did he have to deal with the trial itself, but as the head of the sangha, he had to spend a lot of time on all who came to his temple for help. Yuichi had to tell himself, "My father is not only for me." Yuichi remained hospitalized as the trial carried on. He battled his illness over the coming year, but his condition continued to decline. Shinjo recorded an exchange he had with Yuichi in the hospital:

> When he asked why he was sick all the time, I told him, "Your experience will benefit those to whom you will give counsel. So the buddhas have you going through many hardships. I know it's so hard and so painful. Experiences are sometimes harsh. But, Yuichi, these painful experiences are important."

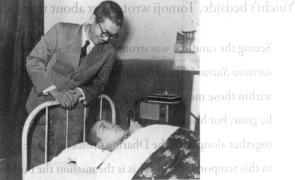

One of the limited occasions of Shinjo being able to visit his son Yuichi at Juntendo Hospital

Shinjo struggled to make sense of it all, as any parent would:

Our son's condition is getting worse. But when he smiles at us in the hospital room, we feel happy. Every second, there is change, there is transition. Each and every passing moment is precious. It brings joy. It is painful and sad, but there are moments of joy and happiness.

The poems Shinjo wrote during these months also express his anguish:

The arm his mother holds has become thin and frail;
only his hand remains firm and strong.
No doubt he yearns for me to stay just a little longer,
yet I tell my beloved son I must go to perform the homa,
    and he nods.
Emotions swell my heart.

Yuichi's condition turned critical on June 28, 1952. As soon as he had concluded the evening homa, Shinjo rushed to the hospital. There was a blackout that night, so a candle had been placed at Yuichi's bedside. Tomoji wrote later about that evening:

Seeing the candle, I was strongly reminded of a passage in the *Mahaparinirvana Sutra*: "A lit candle burns away with each passing moment, yet within those moments it dispels the darkness." Yuichi's body would soon be gone, but his soul would surely join Chibun's and they would work together along with the Dharma protectors to be a guidepost for people in this temporal world. This is the mission the buddhas had given them. I said this to myself, but the thought of losing both sons during our spiritual quest was almost too hard to bear. Unable to utter a word, Shinjo and I stayed up all night at the bedside of our son, who was no longer conscious.

Yuichi fell into a coma. Tomoji spoke to him: "Yuichi, you are now going to where Chibun is. You are returning to where Achala is. You were born on April 8 and share the same birthday with Shakyamuni Buddha. You understand, don't you? Be brave, for you are a man. Your father and mother are going there too." Even though Yuichi was in a coma, one of Shinjo's students witnessed tears falling from his eyes. At 6:55 a.m. the following day, on July 2, 1952, Yuichi passed away at the age of fifteen. Sixteen years before, Shinjo had lost his first son, and now, as the Dharma Crisis dragged on, he lost his second son. A diary entry records Shinjo's thoughts as a parent:

> Sitting at his bedside on the night of the wake, I offered a father's words to a son who would no longer speak: "Yuichi, you are finally back home. We'll stay together tonight. When you were sick in the hospital, I was so busy dealing with the Dharma Crisis that I couldn't really do anything for you. But tonight, I'll stay with you all night.

Yuichi's funeral was held at Shinchoji on July 4. Shinjo gave him the posthumous Dharma name *Shindoin* (One Who Guides to True Practice). At the same time, he gave Chibun the Dharma name *Kyodoin* (One Who Guides to the Teachings).

Bringing the Crisis to a Close and Beginning Anew

As Shinjo grappled with the drawn-out court process of the Dharma Crisis and coped with Yuichi's failing health, he was determined to preserve the teachings and to make a fresh start for the sangha. With this aim in mind, he resigned his position as head of the order and began the process of reorganizing and reforming the community, giving Tomoji his title and formal leadership role. As part of the process of renewal, in 1951 Shinjo decided to change the name of the sangha to "Shinnyo-en."

It is true that the postwar Religious Corporations Ordinance guaranteed freedom of religion in Japan, but religious organizations were still required to register with the government under the 1951 Religious Corporation Act. In 1952, after time-consuming preparation, Shinjo submitted paperwork, just before Yuichi passed away, to the Ministry of Education to have Shinnyo-en legally certified as a religious corporation. News that the application had been accepted came, and as if he were relieved, Yuichi fell into a deep sleep. Although Shinjo was still entangled in a court case and there was great uncertainty about the future of the community, the acceptance of the application to have Shinnyo-en legally recognized was considered a major victory. Of the more than seven hundred applications for recognition submitted to the Ministry of Education that year, only about three hundred were deemed complete and accepted, and of those, only fifty-two were ultimately approved.

On May 16, 1953, ten months after Yuichi's passing, Shinjo received word that the Minister of Education had certified Shinnyo-en as a religious corporation. Four days later Shinnyo-en was successfully registered with the government. The religious community that Shinjo and Tomoji had spent so much time and energy building for nearly two decades had been spared dissolution. It was a great relief to the community that they did not need to wait for the Tokyo High Court to conclude Shinjo's case, which wouldn't happen until the following year.

By January 1954, it had become clear during the trial that Shinjo had neither witnessed nor instigated the incident in the practice hall that the plaintiff had described. Nevertheless, although it had become obvious to all that Shinjo was innocent of the charges of abuse levied against him, he was still given a suspended sentence of seven months' imprisonment and three years' probation. The sentence was handed down, despite the fact that Shinjo was not present or involved in the incident, because the court determined that he bore responsibility as leader of the community.

On the one hand, that any sentence was handed down in the case illustrates the lingering postwar suspicion toward religious organizations. On the other hand, that the sentence was suspended and the Sangha of Truth was granted permission to continue under a new name suggests that the extreme public backlash against religious groups following the war was finally beginning to abate. A decade later in the 1963 "Report on Postwar Changes to Religion and Its Relationship to Society" published by the Federation of New Religious Organizations of Japan, the following was written about Shinjo's case:

> The fact is that the defendant should have been found "not guilty." However, the social climate had led people to place such an emphasis on the rights of the individual that any plea concerning a civil rights violation, no matter how outlandish, would be heard by the courts. Under these circumstances, the head of the Sangha of Truth was found guilty of abuse for using only negligible force during sesshin training. The sangha was permitted to continue, but under a different name. This case clearly exemplifies the prevailing attitude in postwar Japan: the police, the media, and the public branded all new religious organizations as evil and subjected them to persecution without investigating the actual reality.

Luckily Shinjo did not need to wait for his exoneration to begin his religious work anew. Shinnyo-en represented a new beginning in more ways than just a change of name. Shinjo persevered through two simultaneous calamities: being unjustly and publicly accused of a crime by a once-close disciple and losing his beloved fifteen-year-old son. These trying events profoundly affected Shinjo, as they would have anyone. But for Shinjo they had a uniquely profound influence on the development of the system of teaching and practice that he had been shaping for many years.

Struggling to Practice Forgiveness

An issue that weighed heavily on Shinjo's mind was how he could reconcile his feeling of having been betrayed by his trusted disciple with his practice. He had never been so deeply hurt and betrayed by a disciple before. Shinjo's diaries from this period show that he struggled with his feelings toward the student. He had trusted him, but the man had caused serious harm to the community and to Shinjo personally. There are some mentions of the man preserved in Shinjo's writings that predate his 1950 arrest.

In July 1950, about a month before he was arrested, Shinjo mentions that his former disciple had written him a letter in which he defended himself against the charge of behaving inappropriately toward a female student. "His conduct is pathetic," Shinjo wrote regretfully, "but my determination to help him is unshaken."

Shinjo hoped that he would repent and atone for his actions. In Buddhism, to repent means to acknowledge one's misdeeds, to regret having done them, and to ask for forgiveness. The practice can take many forms, depending on the Buddhist denomination. Shinjo wrote in his diary exactly what he said to the disciple when he asked Shinjo if he could repent:

> Let me, when the time comes, hear your remorse through your actions. As for your actual words of contrition, let me hear them only in your final moments. Let your actions speak of your penitence. Only then will you be able to swear to your renewed conscience with words.

The young man replied, "You will definitely have your answer after I have passed away." At that moment, Shinjo wrote, his eyes were shining.

This shows the high hopes Shinjo had for this young man. He was clearly still hoping that he would repent for his behavior. This disciple had already been ordained, so the most important thing was for he himself to repent and atone, not for Shinjo to forgive him. Forgiving him was not the point, Shinjo believed. The man would have to make up for his transgressions through his own deeds, through the conduct he engaged in the rest of his life. After Shinjo was arrested and jailed, he wrote the following in his diary about this disciple in whom he had placed so much trust:

> Wanting to help him, I even put him before my own son. But my effort still fell short. I know my own hardship is just beginning . . . all I can do is to meditate on the great loving-kindness of the buddhas, and may it grant me strength to carry through with my effort.

Elsewhere, Shinjo records portions of his own interrogation at the hands of the prosecutor at the Hachioji District Court. The prosecutor asks Shinjo about his former disciple's affair with a female member of the community, and whether Shinjo holds any hatred or grudge against him. Shinjo clearly states that he never felt that way. On a nearby page of the same diary, we see Shinjo struggling to find inspiration in lines from classic texts and scriptures that will help him make sense of the situation in relation to his own personal practice:

- One should first look at oneself before laying the blame on the other.
- Know the faults in those you love; know the strengths in those you hate.
- Among all beings, honor those who are capable of reflection.
- Bodhisattvas bear all that is unwholesome with fortitude and patience.
- Show equanimity toward all beings, yet be as immovable as the great earth.
- Burden yourself with what others would rather not carry, and give to others that which is more desirable.[22]

Shinjo seems to be admonishing himself with the selected passages. These passages also suggest that he felt it part of his personal practice to not harbor anger toward even those who had harmed him.

---

22. These lines are taken, respectively, from the Neo-Confucian philosopher Zhang Zai; The Book of Rites (Liji), one of the five Chinese classics; The Numerical Discourses of the Buddha (Anguttara Nikaya); *The Garland Sutra* (*Avatamsaka Sutra*); and the *Mahavamsa*, a Pali chronicle of the history of Buddhism.

His notes show that he was reflecting on where he had fallen short and understood that he needed to maintain equanimity toward his former disciple, even if it meant bearing a terrible burden himself.

Shinjo's personal experience of struggling to find forgiveness within himself would stick with him. It may have been this experience that prompted him to search for a robust scriptural basis for the notion that even those who have done the gravest wrong can be rescued from their state and led to enlightenment. "Is there no doctrine that can help all beings?" he asked himself. Shinjo continued to study one sutra after another in search of a systematic set of teachings that did precisely that.

12

Reaping the Fruits of Philosophy and Practice

Searching for a Teaching That Gives Hope to the Hopeless

Shinjo firmly believed that all people could discover their innate buddha nature regardless of the life they had been born into or what they had done in the past. After all, the Buddha himself explicitly rejected the notion that one's station of birth meant anything at all when it came to one's potential for enlightenment. "One does not become a lowly person by birth," he said. "By actions one becomes a lowly person, and by actions one also becomes a brahman."[23]

One of the Buddha's great disciples was a man named Upali, who had been born into a low caste. He was not allowed to be educated. Given his station, Upali made his living as a barber, work that was considered quite lowly in ancient India. According to Buddhist legend, the Buddha first taught Upali meditation as he cut Shakyamuni's hair.

Upali became a monk and quickly mastered the four states of meditative absorption. He became known for his precise knowledge and adherence to the monastic precepts. Some of the other monks

---

23. A well-known line from the *Suttanipata*.

resented Upali, but the Buddha admonished them that anyone who faithfully observes the precepts is worthy of respect. Shinjo sometimes used Upali as evidence that everyone can overcome the circumstances of their birth through their deeds.

Furthermore, even if we are born into a high-status family but behave badly in our lives, our potential for enlightenment remains undiminished. Buddhism enumerates five terrible deeds that will cause one to plunge into the deepest hell immediately after death: killing one's mother, killing one's father, killing a sage, injuring a buddha, and causing a religious community to break apart.

From Shinjo's perspective, his former disciple had nearly caused the breakup of the Sangha of Truth. Not only had he caused a rupture within the community, but he was so mired in delusion that he couldn't bring himself to repent or repair the harm he had done. Despite being concerned for his disciple because of his bad behavior, Shinjo was convinced that the man could still redeem himself and even attain enlightenment.

As a Dharma teacher and leader of a religious community, it was Shinjo's deepest wish to convey the Dharma to his students in a way that would give them hope and inspire them to persevere in their practice, no matter their birth station or their current situation or what they may have done in the past. His experiences with Yuichi and with his former disciple compelled Shinjo to seek a teaching that would reach and lift up even those who were physically weak (like his son) or who became lost (like his former disciple).

Yuichi had attained such wonderful qualities as a result of his practice, even at such a young age and burdened by illness. His former disciple, by contrast, had doomed himself with his destructive behavior despite his promise to repent and atone. Nevertheless,

Shinjo refused to give up hope that he would mend his ways and take up his practice again. Shinjo knew the great transformative power of the Buddhist path and was convinced that it was available to everyone because of our inborn awakenedness, or buddha nature.

Shinjo's diaries during the early days of Shinnyo-en are filled with references and notes to various sutras, as if he were searching for the perfect teaching to reflect what he had come to personally understand through direct experience and a lifetime of study. He had been an avid reader since childhood, and we can see that around this time he reread the sutras, examining them one by one, looking for an answer.

Singling Out the Nirvana Sutra

Gradually the *Nirvana Sutra*, a collection of teachings that coalesce around the final days of the Buddha's life, came to the fore in Shinjo's search for guiding principles that captured his personal understanding and would best reach those he wished to lead. The sutra is more correctly known as the *Mahayana Mahaparinirvana Sutra*, or the *Mahayana Sutra of Great Perfect Nirvana*, or *Great Parinirvana Sutra*. There is another sutra in the Pali Buddhist canon that Theravada Buddhists use called the *Mahaparinibbana Sutta*, which is similarly set around the final days of the Buddha's life. The Pali sutra, however, is much shorter and is a much more literary account of the Buddha's final days without a great deal of philosophical elaboration.

The original Sanskrit version of the *Nirvana Sutra* has been lost. Only fragments survive today, but the Sanskrit sutra has been preserved in several Chinese and Tibetan translations. Because the Chinese and Tibetan translations vary, scholars speculate that there may have been multiple editions of the original sutra down through the centuries. The Chinese translation of the sutra was transmitted to Japan. Although versions of the text differ somewhat, they share a common, positive presentation of nirvana.

Nirvana is a Sanskrit word that means "a state of being blown out or extinguished," as in the flame of a candle. It is also a metaphor for passing away. It isn't meant to refer simply to death as we ordinarily understand it, but to the ultimate form of cessation that passes beyond all delusion and uncertainty that is characteristic of complete enlightenment. In this sense nirvana is often synonymous with enlightenment. It is the ultimate state to which all Buddhists aspire.

In the Pali sutras, nirvana is a tranquil state that occurs when the physical body and the root of all delusions are extinguished. The Mahayana *Nirvana Sutra* holds that nirvana is a state that is always present, peacefully joyous, absolute, and pure. In this sutra, nirvana doesn't simply mean extinction; it also means the attainment of a state that is permanent and timeless.

Part of the Mahayana *Mahaparinirvana Sutra* in the Chinese canon

This positive presentation of nirvana produces two major themes that run throughout the text: buddhas are ever-present, and all sentient beings possess buddha nature. Certainly these two ideas would have resonated with Shinjo as he worked through the loss of Yuichi and struggled to preserve his own practice with respect to his disciple's betrayal. Perhaps one way to understand Shinjo's thinking on this would be to say that there are always buddhas who embody and express universal truths for the benefit of suffering beings, and that all living beings have the potential to awaken to those truths to become buddhas themselves. Hope is never really lost because buddhas are always there and our potential for awakening can never be diminished.

Understanding That No One Is Ever Truly Lost

A fair amount of text in the *Nirvana Sutra* and other Mahayana sutras is devoted to dealing with the issue of "those who are utterly mired in desire" (*icchantika*). People who are deeply mired in desire can neither let go of worldly desires for pleasure and material things nor listen to anyone who attempts to help them. Such people live their lives solely for self-serving ends and cannot be persuaded to do otherwise. Given that Mahayana Buddhism emphasizes the bodhisattva ideal—that is, striving to achieve enlightenment for the benefit of others—these types of people present a special challenge.

It is generally thought that a person who is utterly mired in desire approaches a state of "absolute wickedness." Unable to feel compassion or love for others, or to listen to the wise words of enlightened beings, how could such a person even come close to awakening and attaining buddhahood? Many sutras consider people who are utterly mired in desire as being hopeless cases, unredeemable in a sense. The *Nirvana Sutra* describes those who are utterly mired in desire as having an incurable illness—they lack trust in buddhas and their enlightenment and have severed all the wholesome roots for attaining enlightenment or nirvana. But the sutra also contains the following passage from the chapter "The Nature of Tathagatas":

> The nature of one mired in desire is indeterminate. He continues to commit grave sins, but it isn't true that he cannot take up the buddha path to awakening. The reason is that the moment one who is utterly mired in desire arouses even a little faith in Buddhadharma, he is no longer utterly mired in desire. Also, if he takes up the path to awakening, he is no longer utterly mired in desire. Even those who commit grave transgressions can become buddhas by counteracting them with positive action. No matter what a person does, it does not mean that he cannot achieve awakening at some point in the future.

If the *Nirvana Sutra* intended to teach that those who are mired in desire cannot attain enlightenment, it would not have included this passage. According to the *Nirvana Sutra*, liberation is possible even for those who have cut away all wholesome roots from within, who do wrong because they lack merit, or who commit atrocious acts and renounce faith.

There is a passage in the *Nirvana Sutra* that records a conversation between the Buddha and King Ajatashatru. When he was still a prince, Ajatashatru imprisoned his father, starved him to death, and seized the throne. From a Buddhist point of view, he had committed one of the five deadly sins, which would lead to his plunging into the deepest hell immediately after his death.

After Ajatashatru had committed terrible atrocities against his father and mother, boils broke out all over his body. Reflecting on this, he believed himself to be a depraved person utterly mired in desire. Nevertheless, when the Buddha taught him the Dharma, Ajatashatru became his student. When he expressed to the Buddha his belief that it was inevitable that he would be plunged into the deepest hell upon his death, the Buddha said, "The nature and form of everything related to your body is impermanent. Not one part of it endures. Therefore, Great King, why do you believe that you must be plunged into the deepest hell?" ("Pure Acts")

All phenomena are impermanent by nature. Nothing in this world is fixed, so even an utterly depraved person, if he arouses trust in buddhahood, will cease to be utterly depraved and can become awakened himself. Shinjo came to believe that the *Nirvana Sutra* preached the possibility of buddhahood for all living beings in the truest sense of the idea. His way of thinking, in which we seek the path and realize that we already possess buddhahood within, shares much in common with Kukai's *The Meaning of Becoming a Buddha in This Very Body*.

Shinjo's interest in bringing those who had become far removed from awakening, even by their own reprehensible behavior, onto the path to awakening also calls to mind the image of Mahavairochana, who assumes the wrathful guise of Achala to wrest intransigent beings onto the path. The hope-filled teachings of the *Nirvana Sutra* proved beneficial to Shinjo's thinking as it continued to develop.

Shinjo had already formulated a well-grounded view of Buddhism, but the *Nirvana Sutra* gave him even a clearer direction and form. His systematic presentation was becoming clear: buddhahood is ever-present, and all living things possess buddha

Shinjo in his study at Shinchoji temple

nature. By taking refuge in ever-present buddhahood, one awakens to one's own buddha nature. Cultivating and developing this buddha nature leads one to arrive at the originally pure self within, and this possibility is not closed even to those who are utterly mired in desire.

13.

Creating Art to Awaken the
Buddha in Others

Deciding to Sculpt a Reclining Buddha

In late 1956, Shinjo decided to sculpt an image of the reclining Buddha as he looked while teaching his disciples for the last time. Shinjo had already established the *Nirvana Sutra* as the doctrinal foundation of Shinnyo-en and wanted to create a work that would express the state of great perfect enlightenment. He clearly expresses his thinking on this subject in an article published in *Bunka Jiho* (The Culture Bulletin) in 1962:

> Incidentally, I have been working on sculpting nirvana images since 1957.
> Over the course of three months I sculpted my first one of roughly 16 feet,
> then one that was 9 feet, and then one that was 6 feet. I sculpted them
> wishing to honor the teachings and realizations of all the buddhas.
> . . . There was one Buddhist text in particular that gave me a strong
> sense of certainty with regard to moving forward with my grand project. It
> was, in fact, an excerpt from the chapter "On the Nature of Tathagatas" in
> the *Mahaparinirvana Sutra*, a compilation of Buddhist texts I quite confi-
> dently believe to be most supreme. The excerpt is as follows:

I shall become a stupa—a reminder of buddhahood for other sentient beings to venerate and a representation of the dharma body for them to return to.

Chancing upon the *Nirvana Sutra*, which is considered to be the final teachings that Shakyamuni Buddha left as his will and testament, I read the following in the chapter "Bodhisattva Highly Virtuous King":

The merit of hearing Dharma is what produces great perfect enlightenment. It is because of this merit that all sentient beings acquire the roots of faith.

In addition to this, the following principles are considered to be overall themes of this sacred scripture: all beings have buddha nature, permanence-bliss-self-purity, and even those who are utterly mired in desire can become buddhas.

I thought that rather than embellish these teachings, I should work to embody them in my own life. Right there and then, I found the motivation and conviction to sculpt the nirvana image, and acting on that conviction, I decided to literally and figuratively take off my Buddhist garb. I was ready to simply practice the path. Of course, I continue to respect and honor the Buddhist tradition, but I strongly believe that what truly makes us whole as individuals is an aspiration and practice of the path that honors its most intrinsic, truest intent right alongside and among the people of our own time and place.

Creating a buddha image is not about sculpting form. I am a practitioner of the bodhisattva path dedicated to embodying the Dharma. I must always consider my work to be reverence for and cultivation of the buddha nature in all beings. We may live in a society wherein moral principles are not discussed much, but when we awaken to the buddha nature that exists within each of us, as the above lines from "On the Nature of Tathagatas" urge, we will ourselves see how we ought to live. Eventually, through every experience in life, so many of us will find a truly happy life both physically and spiritually. We will then rejoice with buddhas. I firmly believe that such a realm is possible in this real world.

For the Dharma to manifest correctly, I will first deepen my understanding of what the Buddhist path really is, what it's for, and will help others to know it. With this in mind, I will continue to create images of nirvana throughout my life and will work to inspire both myself and others to be "living buddhas."

Shinjo copied the text of this article into a Japanese-style bound book by hand with a writing brush, which suggests how important

Shinjo and Tomoji with members of their sangha who helped them create the nirvana image

it was to him. For Shinjo, the true purpose of Buddhism is to "shape buddhas in ourselves and others." Sculpting an image of a buddha wasn't about creating a physical, artistic representation of a buddha, but rather about creating a personification of a buddha's awakening. Shinjo's sculpting of buddhas illustrated his resolve to help his students express the buddha nature that dwells within them. In a way, Shinjo created art to make his students into living buddhas.

Sculpting, Installing, and Consecrating the Massive Image

Shinjo decided to sculpt the nirvana statue in November 1956, and within a month had created a scale model. Shortly after the first of the year he began carving in earnest, working night and day, ignoring the winter chill. He had difficulty obtaining the large quantity of clay he required all at once, so he divided the piece into three sections and worked on them one at a time so he could reuse the leftover clay. Shinjo had help from his students, including one who was a master carpenter. But none of them had any experience in sculpting. Nevertheless, the work was completed in ninety days, a remarkable speed for a work of this magnitude.

Although Shinjo had no formal training as a sculptor, as far back as 1937 he had created a relief of an image of Achala in half-lotus position. His duties to the sangha over the next twenty years had prevented him from completing many other works, save for a few plaques and a tablet engraved with the characters for Chiryu Gakuin, the community's Dharma school. Yet, even during those years Shinjo never put down his chisel altogether. With a few small works now and then he occasionally had the opportunity to practice his skills.

Shinjo and members of his sangha creating the nirvana image,
January 27, 1957

In May 1957 Shinjo's reclining Buddha was installed in the Sesshin Training Hall[24] in Tachikawa. He named the work "Ever-
Present Shakyamuni Tathagata." His title brings together three distinct ideas: ever-presence, Shakyamuni, and tathagata. "Shakyamuni," or Sage of the Shakyas, is an epithet for the historical Buddha,
whereas "tathagata" refers to the Buddha's dharma body. Shinjo created the statue to express the idea that the historical Buddha, as
depicted in the *Nirvana Sutra*, is also a tathagata that is by nature the
dharma body. The Dharma that Shakyamuni Tathagata embodies is
"ever-present."

---

24. Shinnyo-en's first expansion of the facilities at its head temple complex.

The completed nirvana image inside the Sesshin Training Hall

The ceremony to consecrate and inspirit the statue was held on November 3, 1957. Shuten Oishi, director of the Federation of New Religious Organizations in Japan, explained how priests over the years had created numerous images of buddhas, bodhisattvas, Dharma protectors, and mandalas that were not only priceless works of art but also invaluable expressions of faith that connect people with buddhas:

> With the passing of time, however, the once-customary devotional practice of image-making among Buddhist priests has faded and primarily become the work of professional artists, who may not share quite the same strong religious commitment. Although their works may have value as art, I am rather skeptical about their spiritual worth for people seeking to revere the buddha spirit within such images. Founders of Buddhist schools such as Master Kobo and Nichiren are known to have sculpted or painted buddha images. But I know of hardly any other religious founder who has done so since then.

Here at Shinnyo-en, however, you are blessed with a founder and spiritual parent who has dedicated all his being to sculpt this great perfect nirvana image in a most reverent manner. Thus a tradition that virtually disappeared several hundred years ago has been revived.

The Unique Character of Shinjo's Image

Although Shinjo later sculpted more than one hundred Buddhist artworks, this first one would remain the largest of all his works. The nirvana statue that Shinjo completed in 1957 measures 16 feet in length from the head to the toes of the reclining Buddha. At slightly less than 5 meters, it is a standard size for reclining buddhas of this kind.

In most other ways, however, Shinjo's work differs from typical Japanese Buddhist images. Shinjo modeled his Buddha's features on the earliest images of the Buddha, which date from about five hundred years after his death. Only then, as the memory of Shakyamuni grew more distant, did people begin to create images of him, particularly in Gandhara, an ancient kingdom that was situated in what is now northern Pakistan and eastern Afghanistan. Gandharan sculpture is renowned for its combination of the Hellenistic and traditional Indian styles. Its influence spread as far as East Asia in ancient times.

Shinjo's reclining buddha is also unusual in that Shakyamuni's face looks very young. Reclining buddha statues are meant to depict the historical Buddha at the age of eighty, just before he entered nirvana.

Yet Shinjo portrayed him when he first attained enlightenment at the age of thirty-five, as an indication that Shakyamuni's first enlightenment and his final nirvana were not separate. He explained that most nirvana statues of the Buddha depicted him naturalistically in old age, but he wanted to show the Buddha's face as it appeared when he first attained enlightenment. "That is when the Buddha transcended the four kinds of suffering that no person can escape—birth, old age, sickness, and death—and attained a state wherein there is no birth or death, which is why he still lives on today. I wanted to depict the Buddha's face as it looked when he was a young man."

Another noteworthy aspect of the statue is the crown on Shakyamuni's head. Usually images of tathagatas depict them wearing simple robes, with no other ornaments. Mahavairochana is the exception. Although Mahavairochana is a tathagata, he is often depicted like a

Shinjo making final adjustments to his nirvana image, January 1957

bodhisattva, with crown, necklaces, bracelets, and other ornaments that indicate princely status. This is done to make clear that Mahavairochana is a primordial buddha, a personification of Dharma. Shinjo adorned his statue with a simple crown, as he made no distinction between Mahavairochana and Tathagata Shakyamuni. For him Tathagata Shakyamuni and the Dharma were one and the same.

Shinjo's sculpture is also unusual in that almost no other examples of nirvana statues exist with a backing, halo-like nimbus. Shinjo placed several smaller buddha images on this background. These smaller images include three of Mahavairochana as he appears in the Diamond Realm mandala with his hands in the Wisdom Fist Mudra, and two of Mahavairochana as depicted in the Matrix Realm mandala seated with his hands in the Dharma Realm Meditation Mudra.

Six seated images of Amitabha have also been sculpted on the background that extends along the Buddha's body. Both Mahavairochana and Amitabha are closely associated with light. Mahavairochana means "Great One Whose Light Shines Everywhere." Similarly, Amitabha means "One Who Possesses Infinite Light."

The background of Shinjo's statue, endowed with boundless, infinite light, expresses another of Shinjo's central thoughts—the fusion of Mahavairochana, the main buddha of esoteric Buddhism, with Amitabha, one of the principal buddha figures associated with exoteric forms of Buddhist practice. It brings them together and illustrates that the Buddha manifests both a perfect physical body obtained in reward for completing the bodhisattva practices and acquiring the wisdom of a buddha and a mental body of pure Dharma, the truth to which all buddhas are enlightened.

14.

Setting Shinnyo-en Apart

Synthesizing Openly Taught and Esoteric Buddhist Traditions

In developing the Shinnyo-en teachings, Shinjo was forging a new path of practice that combined the openly taught (exoteric) Buddhist teachings presented in sutras with the esoteric Buddhist rituals and other practices that are only accessible via initiation under a qualified master who judges when a disciple is ready to receive them. He was bringing together the profound practices he had mastered in the Shingon tradition and the profound truths that were perfectly expressed in the *Nirvana Sutra*, which he had himself come to understand through personal experience.

In many ways, Shinjo was like the priest Kakuban, who, three hundred years after Kukai, sought to unify Shingon esoteric Buddhism and Pure Land Buddhism under the rubric of the Pure Land of Mysterious Adornment. Shinjo had founded the group that would become Shinnyo-en as a community within the Shingon tradition and later branched off as an independent denomination.

Shinnyo-en is distinguished by its focus on the hope-filled teachings of the *Nirvana Sutra* as well as by sesshin, its unique form of meditation training. Shinjo cultivated both of these features in Shinnyo-en so that his teachings would be of maximum benefit to ordinary laypeople and so that his students would be able to attain the states of meditative absorption that would produce insight and awareness that could transform their lives for the better.

Shinjo hoped to help all people, lay and ordained alike, to develop spiritually, grow as human beings, and improve the world around them. His adoption of the *Nirvana Sutra* and the sculpting of the nirvana image were major turning points in this quest. At last, Shinjo was beginning to meet the challenge of opening up the profound insights he had gained through his own rigorous training to ordinary people who did not have the capacity or opportunity to become a monastic as he had.

Forging a Path for Lay Practice in Everyday Life

Shinjo's deepening study of the *Nirvana Sutra* increased his belief that both monks and lay practitioners could walk the path to buddhahood if they had truly developed the aspiration for enlightenment. Throughout most of his teaching career up to that point, Shinjo had occupied the role of a monastic guiding his lay followers in their practice.

The Buddha himself had occupied the same role, and this was primarily the way that Buddhism had been passed down through the ages. For twenty years Shinjo lived as a monk, dressed only in a monk's robes, and kept his head shaven. But after he began to delve into the *Nirvana Sutra*, he let his hair grow and began wearing secular clothing, except when officiating at formal services.

It may have seemed as though Shinjo had quit being a monk and returned to lay life. But just because he grew his hair and put on a tie doesn't mean he had left the Buddhist path behind. The *Nirvana Sutra* had convinced him that it was possible for everyone, even those who are mired in desire, to attain awakening. There was no reason for him to continue drawing a distinction between lay practitioners and monastics.

Similarly, when he was about to pass away the Buddha accepted an offering of food only from Chunda, one of his lay disciples. This episode, recounted in the *Nirvana Sutra*, was of profound significance to Shinjo as it illustrated the value that the Buddha placed on lay practice. Removing his monastic robes was a concrete way for him to show the world that he believed the ideals of Buddhism and the everyday realities of life were one and the same.

Shinjo speaking to practitioners at the Kansai head temple, May 13, 1964

Shinjo developed a unique meditative practice that perfectly expressed his belief that Buddhist practice and the realities of our everyday lives could be one and the same. From the beginning he conceived of sesshin meditative training as composed of structured and unstructured aspects. The structured aspect of sesshin is formal and takes place at the temple with the help of a spiritual guide. The unstructured aspect of sesshin occurs when one brings one's contemplation into daily life, using it as a training ground.

Four Unique Qualities of Shinnyo-en

By bringing Shingon esoteric Buddhism together with the *Nirvana Sutra*, Shinjo was creating his own Buddhist tradition that incorporated intellectual rigor from a variety of sources, not just from orthodox Buddhism. In fact, some Japanese Buddhists would be startled by those facets and practices in Shinnyo-en that represent a departure from traditional Japanese Buddhism.

First of all, the vocabulary used within Shinnyo-en differs from that of more traditional Buddhist denominations. From childhood, Shinjo was an avid reader. In his diaries, he quotes not only Buddhist texts and other East Asian scriptures but also Western writers like Shakespeare and Descartes. Even after he took up his religious vocation, Shinjo continued to read widely on many topics, including spiritualism, and he often used words that reflected this influence, such as "spiritual powers" and "spiritual realm," which some might consider naive. Since many idiosyncratic terms like these have become part of the vocabulary of Shinnyo-en, others may have the impression that the group somehow betrays traditional Buddhist thinking.

Second, Shinjo understood the common Japanese Buddhist concepts of "self-power" and "other-power" in a unique way. The most popular Japanese Buddhist traditions place a great emphasis on other-power when it comes to practice. That is, practicing means undertaking rituals or performing prayers to petition the aid of buddhas in one's life.

Of course, Shinjo also felt that rituals and prayer were important, too, so in that sense he also valued other-power. But from his point of view, practice consists of becoming aware of our inner buddha nature, polishing it, and attaining a state of enlightenment that is eternal, blissful, absolute, and pure. The purpose of relying on other-power is to help the practitioner polish his or her buddha nature in the world, wherein ordinary, everyday life is the training ground. This means that contrary to what most Japanese Buddhists do, Shinjo emphasized self-power in his teachings.

Third, Shinjo clearly believed that nirvana could be realized in the here and now, right in this world. The *Nirvana Sutra* skillfully lays out the idea that the Buddha is ever-present. The ever-present, unchanging Buddha is essentially his own awakenedness or buddhahood. To attain the same state of awakenedness and to maintain it is the same as being in nirvana, which is itself permanent, blissful, absolute, and pure. Here, Shinjo's thought is similar to Kukai's idea of "buddhahood in this very body." According to Kukai, by reconciling the three actions—body, speech, and mind—of Mahavairochana with those of human beings, we attain buddhahood with this body, just as it is.

Lastly, others may find it strange that Shinjo's deceased sons have become objects of veneration within the community and that community members sometimes pray for their guidance. The loss of his beloved sons had a profound effect on Shinjo's religious development. He threw himself wholeheartedly into Shingon ascetic training after losing little Chibun, and the intense period of spiritual questioning after the passing of Yuichi led him in the end to the *Nirvana Sutra*. That their deaths produced such profound resolution in their father, and that Yuichi exhibited such remarkable spiritual qualities and acumen in his young life, likely inspired the idea that the two boys represented the working of a higher power in Shinjo's life. While Shinjo did not intend for Chibun and Yuichi to become objects of devotion, Shinnyo-en members came to view them in this light.

Regarding the role that his sons came to occupy within the Shinnyo-en community, Shinjo wrote in his diary:

> I have never thought to have my children revered as buddhas. If Kyodoin (Chibun) and Shindoin (Yuichi) can assist others in their process of coming to know the loving compassion of buddhahood or to experience the

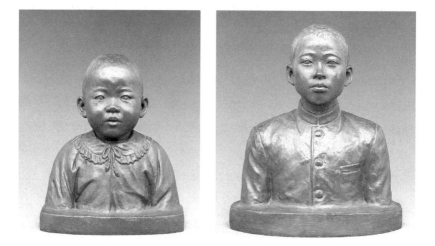

Busts of Chibun and Yuichi sculpted by Shinjo

joys of bodhisattvahood, that, in itself, would be an expression of the work of the buddhas, for which I would only feel thankful. But I have no intention to use them to fixate on a past that cannot be changed.

The Meaning of "Shinnyo-en"

Shinjo intended to offer something uniquely suited to our new age that would nevertheless retain the spirit of esoteric Buddhism. The name that he chose when he restructured his sangha indicated his intentions.

Shinnyo denotes both buddhahood and the true nature of all things—*tathata* in Sanskrit. *Tathata* is a concept central to Buddhist thought, and can be translated quite literally as "thusness" or "suchness." The universal truth of the Dharma is manifest in thusness.

But what is thusness? It is difficult to describe, like trying to explain what an apple tastes like or what your love for another feels like. But we might think of it this way: In the space of a single snap of the fingers, the existence and reality of that moment, with its infinite potential and uniqueness, is already gone. Within the space of a single finger snap is contained the sum of all previous moments stretching back into infinity and the great potential for all as-yet-unimagined future moments stretching forward into infinity. That single moment cannot be what it is without everything that came before and without pouring itself into everything that will come after. It is impossible to conceive of even an instantaneous moment that exists apart from the inexpressible infinite. Everything we could possibly know or experience is thus. Thusness therefore refers to the quality or nature of things being thus.

The word *shinnyo* written by Shinjo as
a gift for one of his students

The Buddha often referred to his own state of awakening in relationship to thusness. Throughout his teaching career, the Buddha called himself "Tathagata." *Tathagata* is a Sanskrit word that can mean both "One Who Has Come Thus" and "One Who Has Gone

Thus," but which is often read metaphorically to mean "One Who Has Arrived at Suchness or Thusness." Shinjo cited a passage from the *Sutra of Golden Light* to make his understanding of the connection between the Buddha and thusness clear:

> The Buddha does not die. Likewise, the Dharma does not perish. The Buddha is going to leave this earthly existence in order to benefit people. The Buddha is wondrous and mysterious. . . . The substance of buddhas is suchness (*shinnyo*). Thusness is none other than the One Who Has Arrived at Thusness (*Tathagata*)—and is also named *nirvana*.

In *The Light in Each Moment*, Shinjo refers to this quote when explaining his choice of the new name, Shinnyo-en, for his Dharma community: the word *shinnyo* is clarified in the *Sutra of Golden Light* as the unseen "substance." He goes on to say that the character used to render *en* (苑) indicates a borderless garden into which all beings can freely enter.

It was Shinjo's hope that his community would become a "borderless garden" in which everyone was welcomed and made comfortable as they embarked upon the work of discovering shinnyo, or thusness, or their true nature, for themselves. He envisioned a place without borders where all who desire to realize their true natures are welcome. This would be Shinnyo-en.

15

The Flower of Shinnyo-en Blossoms and Shinjo Passes Away

Sharing Shinnyo-en with the World

The 1950s and 1960s were years of tremendous growth for Shinnyo-en. In the decade following the incident with Shinjo's former disciple and the death of his son and successor, Shinjo's religious community had grown steadily in both popularity and stature. In January 1962 Shinnyo-en was recorded as having thirty-five locations and 128,000 members.

In 1966, the year Shinjo turned sixty, a well-known Thai temple announced that it would offer a gift of Shakyamuni Buddha's relics to Shinnyo-en. Relics of the Buddha are very sacred points of focus for Buddhist meditation and prayer. They are the most powerful symbolic reminders of the Buddha's teachings and his presence in our world.

According to the *Nirvana Sutra* in the Pali tradition, the Buddha's body was cremated after his death and his remains were separated into eight urns. Each of these urns were enshrined in a reliquary stupa to commemorate the Buddha in the different geographical communities that had grown up around his teachings. Over time, the relics housed in these stupas were further divided and spread among stupas in even more far-flung communities, like those in Sri Lanka, Myanmar, and Thailand. Many such stupas still occupy a central place as objects of worship in Buddhist temple compounds in these lands.

The Shinnyo-en community held a service to welcome the relics on July 30, 1966, at the Sesshin Training Hall of Shinnyo-en's head temple complex in Tachikawa. Several dignitaries, including Rosen Takashina, chairman of the Japanese Buddhist Federation, were present. Mr. Takashina served as the officiating priest. Venerable Ankro, a member of the Thai contingent that attended the services, shared some of the history of the Buddha relics. He noted that they were brought to Southeast Asia by arhat monks with a wish for a peaceful future for humankind during the reign of King Ashoka of ancient India. He addressed the Shinnyo-en membership: "May you all continue to work toward peace and the benefit of all humanity! Please put into practice the message of buddhas that global peace is possible only through the acknowledgement that the world is one."

To express his gratitude, in November 1966, Shinjo and Tomoji participated in the Eighth International Congress of the World Fellowship of Buddhists in Chiang Mai, Thailand, and personally presented a golden nirvana image that he had sculpted.

After the International Congress, Shinjo and Tomoji stopped in India to undertake a Buddhist pilgrimage prior to returning home. The trip westward from Calcutta to Benares took more than ten hours on an old-fashioned train that had just a few electric fans in place of air conditioning. After another hourlong bus ride from Benares, Shinjo's group eventually made it to Sarnath, the historical location where the Buddha had first "turned the wheel of dharma,"

Shinjo and Tomoji in Chiang Mai, Thailand, November 7, 1966

an eloquent way of referring to the Buddha's first sermon following his enlightenment.

Although all that remained at Sarnath, a once-sprawling Buddhist monastery complex, was just a small portion of its former holdings, Shinjo and his colleagues were overcome with a feeling of deep reverence for the greatness of the Buddha when they imagined the magnificent past of the place. Although the trip had been hastily planned, it left Shinjo with a powerful impression of how truly blessed he was to be able to attain lasting happiness by encountering the Buddha's teachings, despite having been born in Japan.

Shinjo and Tomoji paying respects at Sarnath, India, November 10, 1966

The following year, in 1967, Shinjo and Tomoji organized a delegation representing the Japanese Buddhist communities to promote international goodwill and religious exchange with the West. In a period of less than a month, from June 11 to July 4, they visited nine countries in Europe and the Middle East. "Just as the *Nirvana Sutra* says that each of the eight great rivers eventually reach the same great sea," Shinjo mused, "our missions represent a new dawn for spiritual harmony and for the light that radiates from the nirvana image to shine throughout the world."

Shinjo left Japan in June and returned in July, the memorial months of his sons, Chibun and Yuichi. "This was no coincidence," he later wrote, "as we believed that the two boys were guiding us from the spiritual world."

The delegation's primary mission was to present over one thousand publications, many of which were Buddhist scriptures, as well as an image of the Buddha in nirvana to the University of Oslo in Norway. They also visited two other prestigious institutions: the University of Copenhagen in Denmark and Uppsala University in Sweden. Shinjo presented each institution with commemorative gifts, including a nirvana image.

The group of twenty-five or so Shinnyo-en members then visited Buddhist societies in London and Paris, after which they traveled to Geneva, Switzerland, and the mountain town of Chamonix, France, at the foot of Mont Blanc. In Geneva they visited the World Council of Churches, an ecumenical organization of Protestant and Orthodox churches.

Another highlight of the trip was a visit to the Vatican, where Shinjo and Tomoji had a private audience with Pope Paul VI. Shinjo presented the head of the Roman Catholic Church with an image of

Shinjo and Tomoji visiting the London Buddhist Society, June 22, 1967

the Buddha in nirvana. The Pope, in return, gave Shinjo and Tomoji each an amulet that he had blessed. When Shinjo said, "The teachings of buddhas and the teachings of God share the same goal—the peace and happiness of humankind," the Pope reportedly nodded, clasped Shinjo's hand, and replied, "My special feelings of friendship and trust in Japanese religion have today become firm."

They promised each other that they would work toward their common goal.

That evening, Shinjo recorded a message at the Vatican Broadcasting Bureau where he expressed what is inherently fundamental to the Buddhist path: a spirit of harmony, peace, and inclusivity which was relayed back to Japan. It was the first time a Japanese person had been asked to speak over Vatican Radio and the program provoked an enthusiastic response in Japan.

Before returning home, the delegation visited Hebrew University in Israel.

Losing a Wife, Partner, and
Dharma Friend of Thirty-Five Years

Tomoji began to show signs of exhaustion toward the end of the trip. She pretended that nothing was wrong, but began to spend more and more time alone in prayer and meditation. Shinjo grew concerned. When the group took an excursion to Mont Blanc, he stayed behind at the hotel with Tomoji. They used the time to offer consolatory prayers for the thousands of people who had lost their lives on the mountain.

On June 28, when they had traveled to Rome to visit the Vatican, one of the primary purposes of the trip, Tomoji looked particularly ill. She needed the support of two people just to walk to the audience room. But when the Pope entered, she seemed to suddenly recover her strength. In a strong voice, she asked for permission to take a picture. Taking photographs was normally prohibited, but the Pope granted her request.

The grueling nature of the trip—nine countries were visited in less than three weeks—took a lot out of Tomoji. When they returned from Europe, she took to bed. Three doctors examined her but could find nothing wrong. Shinjo believed she was exhausted as much by spiritual influences she had experienced as by any physical exertion.

Shinjo and Tomoji at a private audience with Pope Paul VI, June 28, 1967

Despite not feeling well, Tomoji continued to attend services with her husband. She did so mostly, Shinjo believed, so people would not worry about her. During the first few days of August she felt well enough to join Shinjo and their daughter Masako at activities at their temple in the Osaka area, including a service on the fourth of the month when she thanked members for their prayers during their trip abroad.

August 6 was the first Sunday of the month. Usually Shinjo and Tomoji would work at the Chiryu Gakuin Dharma school during the morning and then lead a service in the afternoon. But that morning, Tomoji told Shinjo that she had better stay in bed and rest. She insisted, however, that Shinjo keep his commitment to be there for a discussion with their students as he always did.

About two hours later, Masako suddenly rushed in with a worried look on her face and said, "Something is wrong with Mother!" Startled, Shinjo dashed to the second floor to find his wife lying face-down in bed. He detected a faint pulse, so he attempted to revive her using mouth-to-mouth resuscitation. The two rushed to find a doctor, but given that it was a Sunday, it took more than thirty minutes for the doctor to arrive. By the time the doctor arrived, Tomoji had already departed for the next world.

Tomoji, who had been Shinjo's wife, Dharma friend, and cofounder and fellow leader of Shinnyo-en, passed away on the death anniversary of Shobo, the founder of Daigoji. Shinjo had been married to her for thirty-five years. Tomoji was only fifty-five years old at the time of her death.

On August 8, two days after her death, Daigoji, the headquarters of the Daigo school of Shingon Buddhism, bestowed upon Tomoji the posthumous rank of Daisojo, the highest Buddhist priestly rank.

Tomoji had been the first person to practice Shinjo's teachings. Without her early support, Shinnyo-en would not exist.

Following tradition, a memorial service was held every seven days for seven consecutive weeks after Tomoji's death. The common thread throughout all of the eulogies delivered at these services was that Tomoji had demonstrated the essence of the Shinnyo teachings. She exemplified the crucial passage in the *Nirvana Sutra* that teaches us to put the welfare of others before our own. Many Shinnyo-en members adored her and looked on her like a mother.

Shinjo and Tomoji at Kansai Head Temple, November 17, 1965

Shinjo described the way Tomoji lived her life in a verse he composed:

Though my life, like morning dew, may vanish at any time,
I will use this moment to serve others.

Shinjo recounted several stories about Tomoji. One of the stories he shared was about how Tomoji would always return to Tachikawa with a huge sack of sweet corn and tomatoes on her back after every visit to their hometown. He once asked her to stop, saying that she looked like a black-market peddler. She would agree to stop, but after each trip she somehow still managed to bring her bundle onto the train and carry it home by herself.

"She didn't care how she looked," Shinjo explained, "she just wanted our students to eat fresh vegetables."

Realizing the Genesis Temple

When the Sesshin Training Hall was first built it seemed spacious. But as the number of community members increased, it became obvious that something much larger was needed. Often, particularly during the annual festivals, many members had to stand outside in the courtyard.

Plans to build a major expansion were first discussed on March 28, 1966, Shinjo's sixtieth birthday. Construction of the new temple began with a land purification rite on May 31, 1967. In August 1967, after the fourteenth-day memorial service for Tomoji, Shinjo began to sculpt a nirvana image for the new temple.

On May 9, 1968, the roof was completed with a topping-out ceremony and Shinjo completed his nirvana image in June of that year. The largest crowd that ever gathered in the short history of Shinnyo-en celebrated the opening of the new temple on November 2, 1968. The relics received from Thailand had been enshrined in the main altar room along with the statue that Shinjo had sculpted. The ceremonies held to celebrate the opening of the temple were mostly traditional in nature, but wanting to express the spirit of nirvana in a way suited to the current era, Shinjo incorporated lights and music to give the celebration a modern touch.

Shinjo conducting rites in front of the newly consecrated nirvana image

Shinjo's personal memories of the event are filled with poignant recollections of Tomoji. He wrote:

> The more magnificent our buildings and ceremonies became, the more painful it was to think of Tomoji, who had never stepped into the temple she had put her heart into realizing. I wasn't alone in this feeling, as I believe everyone shared the same heartache. I could almost hear her strong, clear chanting voice echoing through the hall.

Spreading Shinnyo-en throughout Japan and the World

After the third memorial of Tomoji's passing in 1970, a flurry of Shinnyo-en temples were opened throughout Japan—fifteen of them between 1970 and 1978.

This period also marked the beginning of Shinjo's outreach to disciples living abroad. In October 1970, Shinjo and his daughter Masako made an eighteen-day trip to the United States, stopping in a number of cities, including San Francisco, where they met with members of Shinnyo-en.

The group of members welcomed Shinjo and Masako at the airport with a bouquet of flowers. In his hotel, Shinjo gave a talk about the inseparability of the Three Jewels, one of the prevailing ideas in the *Nirvana Sutra*, and explained the *Sandai,* one of the most important chants of Shinnyo-en that invokes the power that flows from the inseparability of the Three Jewels. The group chanted together *Namu Shinnyo Ichinyo Dai Hatsu-Nehan Kyo,* expressing the wish to identify with the true nature of reality and to practice the teachings of the *Nirvana Sutra.* Shinjo said, "Whenever you are suffering, or feeling sad, try to chant this *Sandai.*" There were tears all around. Masako urged the group, "Please never forget this moment!"

Many of them didn't. By the time Shinjo returned to San Francisco the following year, there were about fifty members in the city and its suburbs: in Berkeley, Oakland, San Jose, and even as far as Fairfield, near Sacramento.

Shinjo and Masako also visited Los Angeles, Chicago, and Niagara Falls on the same visit in 1970. Their final stop on the trip was Hawaii, where they had a small gathering at the residence of a local member. During this visit, Shinjo visited the *USS Arizona* Memorial.

Offering consolatory prayers for friend and foe without distinction was always critical for him. He felt that this was especially

Shinjo and Masako offering prayers at the *USS Arizona* Memorial, Pearl Harbor

important when it came to those who had lost their lives at Pearl Harbor. In May 1973, Shinjo visited Hawaii again to dedicate the Honolulu temple and for the inspiriting of the nirvana image. Under a bright tropical sun, surrounded by the equally bright green foliage, he prayed for the victims of the Japanese attack on Pearl Harbor and for those laid to rest in the National Memorial Cemetery of the Pacific. Shinjo again expressed his hope that his teachings would reveal the true significance of not distinguishing between friend or foe, and would help build a bridge of renewed friendship between Japan and the United States.

In 1977, with its growing membership and with Shinjo's concerted efforts to reach out to Asia and the rest of the world, Shinnyo-en was formally recognized as a third, distinct form of Japanese esoteric Buddhism. To mark the thirty-fifth anniversary of the founding of Shinchoji, Yushu Okada, the chief abbot of Daigoji, proclaimed that in addition to the old traditions of Shingon and Tendai esoteric Buddhism, Japan now had a third esoteric movement born of the twentieth century called *Shinnyo Mitsu,* or Shinnyo esoteric Buddhism.

In April 1984, Shinjo officiated at ceremonies held at Daigoji to commemorate the 1,150th anniversary of the death of Kukai, the founder of Shingon Buddhism. Over the years, Shinjo had developed a deep relationship with the 101st abbot of Daigoji, Yushu Okada.

In December 1985, Shinjo presented a nirvana image he created to Eiheiji Temple in Fukui, the headquarters of the Soto Zen denomination. Shinjo had become good friends with Rosen Takashina, head of the Soto denomination of Zen at the time. As a sign of his friendship with these two high-ranking monks, Shinjo sculpted busts of both men.

Left: Shinjo and Yushu Okada. *Right*: Shinjo and Tomoji with Rosen Takashina

Passing beyond the World

By his birthday on March 28, 1989, Shinjo was feeling too ill to meet the members of the sangha who gathered to celebrate. Shinjo no longer had the strength to appear in public, so he watched the festivities via a TV monitor.

Shinjo passed away on July 19, 1989. He was eighty-three years old. Looking back on his life, we see a man's remarkable spiritual evolution forged through the immense social and political upheavals of wartime Japan and numerous personal tragedies.

Young Fumiaki Ito had moved from Yamanashi to Tokyo when he was just seventeen. He married Tomoji at twenty-six, and at the age of twenty-nine he obtained the statue of Achala carved by Unkei. The following year he adopted the religious name Tensei and resigned from his job as an aircraft engineer to pursue his religious vocation full time. That same year he was ordained at Daigoji and became a monk.

At age thirty-two, he founded the Tachikawa Fellowship of Achala as a branch temple of the Daigo denomination of Shingon and was

Shinjo at Shinnyo-en's head temple (1985)

given the Buddhist name Shinjo. At thirty-three he completed the Ein transmission in the Shugendo tradition, and at thirty-five he was appointed acting head priest of the old historic temple Johoin. By the following year, he had mastered the core teachings and practices of Shingon esoteric Buddhism and was initiated into the Dharma transmission rite of the Diamond and Matrix Realm mandalas.

After the Second World War, Shinjo led his group to become independent of the Shingon denomination, and he changed the name of his group from the Fellowship of Achala to the Sangha of Truth.

Along the way, he supported his growing family, struggled with poverty, was jailed on dubious charges, and bore the untimely deaths of his two beloved sons and wife, his spiritual partner of thirty-five years. From the peril of crisis within his community, he forged his group anew under the name "Shinnyo-en" and poured all his energy into creating a spiritual tradition that could flourish and spread far and wide to as many people as possible throughout the world.

Such is the story of the life and thought of Shinjo Ito, a Buddhist who lived during Japan's Showa era, and who founded a new Buddhist path. He brought the words of Shakyamuni Buddha to everything in his life:

Transient are all component things. Strive on with diligence.

Epilogue

Shinjo's Lineage Endures

OF THE SIX CHILDREN THAT Shinjo and Tomoji had, only their third daughter, Masako, received a name that used the first character of Shinjo's name. In 1983, Masako completed the Shinnyo Samaya Dharma transmission and Shinjo gave her the Dharma name *Shinso*.

In 1984, five years before Shinjo's passing, he publicly announced Shinso as his most accomplished disciple and Dharma successor. She

Shinjo and Shinso at the Daigoji Monastery officiating
at Kukai's 1,150th memorial service, April 24, 1984

has since kept the spirit Shinjo instilled in Shinnyo-en alive. While drawing inspiration from Buddhist tradition, with awareness that the teachings must be meaningful for people living today, she has taught an engaged form of Buddhism that guides both the individual and Shinnyo-en as a whole.

In recent years, in addition to teaching Shinnyo-en practitioners throughout the world, Shinso has conducted ceremonies dedicated to peace and harmony between cultures and religions. Acting on her belief that all life is interconnected, she has partnered with secular philanthropic foundations throughout the world. She is committed, together with her sangha members, to providing disaster relief, humanitarian and medical aid, social protection, and educational aid, and to the preservation of traditional culture and the promotion of innovative artistic and cultural programs. Shinjo's spirit of creative engagement with the world in myriad forms lives on today through his heir.

Afterword

Harmony amid Diversity

THE FACT THAT *SHINJO* WAS published by Chuokoron-Shinsha just prior to this English edition is deeply moving because Chuokoron originated with the periodical *Hanseikai Zasshi* (Magazine of the Reflection Society) after the shock of the anti-Buddhist movement in the Meiji era (1868–1912). This magazine for the Buddhist revival movement sought to clothe itself in modernity, comparative thought, and spiritualism. One of the key founding members of the first issue was the Buddhist studies and Sanskrit scholar Junjiro Takakusu (1866–1945). The enormous task of compiling the Taisho Tripitaka, which comprises the Chinese Buddhist canon and its Japanese commentaries, now continues as a digital archive project led by Professor Masahiro Shimoda of the University of Tokyo. Shinnyo-en is engaged in supporting this important endeavor.

The Venerable Egen Saeki (1873–1951), former chief abbot of the Daigoji Monastery of the Shingon tradition and a direct Buddhist master of Shinjo in his Dharma transmission, is known to have been greatly influenced by Professor Takakusu during his studies at the University of Tokyo's Department of Indian Philosophy. Stimulated by the current of the renewed Buddhist movement promoted by groups such as the collaborators of *Hanseikai* magazine, Daigoji chief abbot Saeki expressed esoteric Buddhist ideas in the new vernacular of that time while also drawing on Western philosophy and mysticism.

As a leader in esoteric Buddhism, Saeki demonstrated his openness of mind by going beyond the boundaries of the Sanboin stream of Daigoji in doctrine and ritual while not being bound by inter-denominational differences or fixed identities. This can be seen in his receiving teachings from and having a close relationship with the acharya Horyu Doki (1854–1923) of the Shingon Omuro school, who is known for his frequent correspondence with Kumagusu Minakata, a naturalist and folklorist and Japan's first ecologist.

In this line of events, the encounter between chief abbot Saeki and Shinjo was, you might say, predestined. Before Shinjo encountered Shingon esoteric Buddhism, he embarked on a lengthy odyssey that led him through the study of divination practices in his youth, mystical experiences with Zen and Shugendo, experimentation with sectarian Shinto and Unitarian Christianity, and encounters with the mysteries of the spiritual gifts that Tomoji possessed that had historically been passed down through women in her family.

Shinjo was also interested in the Western perspective on human history since ancient times and possessed an aeronautical engineer's scientific knowledge and methodology. The chief abbot felt a deep sympathy with Shinjo and selected this "outsider" (people viewed him as such, as he was not born into a line of priests from a traditional Buddhist sect) to be his direct disciple. He instructed Shinjo in the traditions of the Diamond and Matrix Realm mandalas, and transmitted his Dharma lineage to him with great zeal. The connection between them calls to mind Huiguo's (746–805) initiation of Kukai (774–835) into his lineage of esoteric Buddhism.

"Those who master these teachings are qualified to start a new sect." With this statement Saeki communicated his hope that Shinjo would complete the work that he had not been able to do because of the limitations of that time, by developing a new platform for esoteric Buddhist teachings and practice.

While Shinjo cherished his teacher's kindness, he also felt that the thinking of the scholar Takakusu and the chief abbot Saeki tended toward "monism" and saw the possible danger of a tendency to self-righteousness. All people, religions, and ideas come together on a fundamental level. Yet the unique character, spiritual features, and history of each is to be respected and affirmed, and the pluralism that allows each to flourish is essential. Unity is none other than diversity: for Shinjo this was the meaning of *shinnyo*. For many years Shinjo and Tomoji studied the flower of shinnyo that opens into the beauty of diversity and led people to experience the fruition of shinnyo within themselves.

The *Nirvana Sutra* principles of timelessness and buddha nature expound the esoteric truth of shinnyo, the truth of believing in the unity of all diversity. Shinjo and Tomoji explored ways to express shinnyo. The artistic creation of sculptures, altruistic communal practices, and offering prayers to be in oneness with the life force that encompasses past, present, and future are such examples. They worked to kindle the inextinguishable light of goodness in the hearts of all people without bounds. The new mantra they established— *Namu Shinnyo Ichinyo Dai Hatsu-Nehan Kyo*—also expressed this truth. This mantra, unique to Shinnyo-en, expresses the wish to identify with the true nature of reality and practice the teachings of the *Nirvana Sutra*. It also emphasizes the unity of the Three Jewels.

Shinjo passed away on July 19, 1989. Like the description in the *Nirvana Sutra* of the Buddha Shakyamuni's passing 2,500 years ago, a beautiful full moon was shining that night in 1989 as well. His passing has helped us who practice the Shinnyo path and uphold the *Nirvana Sutra* to truly experience a presence that is timeless. It is always there, like the constant light of the sun and moon, which continues to shine no matter how heavily clouds may sometimes cloak the sky. Each day as we wholeheartedly chant *Namu Shinnyo*, we renew our vow to embody the truths of shinnyo.

I firmly believe that through our endeavors to engage in practice and through selfless acts, the harmony amid diversity that Shinjo so longed to see will become a wider reality in the world.

—Her Holiness Shinso Ito

About the Author

KIDO, known as the "far north poet," has published several poetry books and essays and is one of the most important poets on the front line of contemporary poetry in Japan. He has translated many English poems into Japanese and has introduced works by Ezra Pound and T. S. Eliot to Japan. Kido has been a critic and columnist for various magazines and newspapers and has a profound knowledge of Japanese culture.

About Wisdom Publications

Wisdom Publications is the leading publisher of classic and contemporary Buddhist books and practical works on mindfulness. To learn more about us or to explore our other books, please visit our website at wisdompubs.org or contact us at the address below.

Wisdom Publications
199 Elm Street
Somerville, MA 02144 USA

We are a 501(c)(3) organization, and donations in support of our mission are tax deductible.

Wisdom Publications is affiliated with the Foundation for the Preservation of the Mahayana Tradition (FPMT).